Why Your Depression Isn't Getting Better

Fallen Angels

Terence West

ISBN: 0-75961-369-9

This book is printed on acid free paper.

1stBooks – rev. 3/7/01

Why Your Depression Isn't Getting Better

The Epidemic of Undiagnosed Bipolar Disorders

Michael R. Bartos, M.D.

Writers Club Press
San Jose New York Lincoln Shanghai

Why Your Depression Isn't Getting Better
The Epidemic of Undiagnosed Bipolar Disorders

Writers Club Press
an imprint of iUniverse.com, Inc.

For information address:
iUniverse.com, Inc.
620 North 48th Street, Suite 201
Lincoln, NE 68504-3467
www.iuniverse.com

All names and superficial details have been altered to preserve the confidentiality of all individuals and the organizations whose cases are discussed herein.

****

This book is not intended as a substitute for the medical advice of physicians. The reader should regularly consult a physician in matters relating to his or her health. and particularly with respect to any symptoms that may require diagnosis or medical attention.

ISBN: 0-595-12209-4

Printed in the United States of America

"The wind blows, and restless are the sails;
Even the rudder begs direction;
Yet quietly my captain awaits my silence."
                                    —Kahlil Gibran

Table of Contents

Acknowledgment

Thanks goes out to the many people who helped inspire me and make this book possible.

First and foremost are the patients themselves who had to endure their illness with courage and dignity, and frequently with patience as we waited together for treatment to begin working.

Long overdue thanks to Oliver Bjorksten, MD in Charleston, SC who first got me thinking about bipolar spectrum disorders back in the mid 1980's. Also thanks to Dr. Hagop Akiskal whose work has been a grand inspiration. I met him only once at a conference, and he was kind enough to send me a stack of his articles which led to further inquiries of my own. The Therapeutic Review Committee at Napa State Hospital in the early 1990's provided a forum for reflection and support on developing further ideas.

I appreciate the technical support from Nancy Welch who spent close to a year transcribing the original rough drafts, and Dona Bakker who did the final drafts. Special thanks go to Susie and Chuck Ryan who run the Strawberry Valley Inn at Mt. Shasta, California for providing an idyllic and peaceful environment for writing and relaxing.

There are numerous colleagues and friends who looked over the manuscripts and provided helpful comments including John Arden, PhD, Caye Brookshire, MD, Steve Priebe, PhD, Ian Osborn, MD, and Judy O'Dea, RN.

And thanks to you, Mom, for coming up with a title much catchier than my original one.

Introduction

Do You Have a Bipolar Spectrum Disorder?
The Clues

1. Depression started during your teen years.
2. One or both of your parents were substance abusers.
3. Depression and irritability are part of your family tree.
4. There is a family history of completed suicide.
5. Sometimes you need a lot of sleep while other times you can get by on just a few hours.
6. You've been divorced three times by age 40.
7. You had serious postpartum depression.
8. You don't like the taste of alcohol, but it is the only way you can calm down.
9. Sometimes you feel better than well.
10. Your credit cards are charged to the max (and it was stuff you really didn't need).
11. You have too many speeding tickets.
12. You feel like you have a motor running in your body.
13. Your thoughts go so fast; you don't know what you're thinking.
14. At night, your mind is like a movie, you wish you could just turn off.
15. You start a lot of projects, but when your energy goes down, you can't finish any of them.

16. Sometimes your temper flares up out of nowhere. You throw and break things.

17. Antidepressants make you feel hyper or spacey or even more depressed.

18. You eat and sleep more when you are depressed.

19. Sometimes you get chatty and run up big (really big) phone bills.

20. You change jobs frequently.

21. Winter makes you seriously depressed.

22. People used to come to you to get things done, but now you don't feel like you can do anything.

23. You've been sent for drug and alcohol counseling, but you know your problems are deeper than that.

24. You have mood swings.

25. You work longer hours than you really need to.

26. You have relatives with thyroid disease.

27. You travel impulsively.

28. You gamble excessively.

29. When you get depressed, you get really nervous and agitated too.

30. The doctors keep giving you pills but can't figure out why your depression isn't getting better.

Our libraries and book stores have literally hundreds of books on the shelves related to the topic of depression. These books approach the understanding and treatment of depression from social, psychological and medical perspectives. However, there are no books which focus strictly on the concept of clinical depression which has its roots in bipolar disorders. Until recently, bipolar depression was considered to be the down side of manic depressive illness. Over the last decade there has been an explosion in the amount of research on this topic. Hundreds of articles have appeared in the psychiatric literature concerning the nature and prevalence of this rather common form of depression. Recent information from the National Institute of Mental Health, the American Psychiatric Association, and numerous universities and research facilities has indicated that depression with its roots in bipolar disorder is much more common than ever thought. Perhaps three to five percent of the general population is at risk for a bipolar depression. Up to half of all clinical depressions may be bipolar in nature. Bipolar depressions are massively underdiagnosed and mistreated. Agitation, irritability and, even worse, depression often result from what appears to be improper treatment. Although current research is shedding light on the problem of misdiagnosed depression, mental health professionals are still rather slow to catch on and continue to misdiagnose and mistreat this now recognized common form of depression. The use of common antidepressants generally causes worsening of bipolar depression. The term "bipolar spectrum" refers to the large variety of ways bipolar depression often presents. The majority of patients with this disorder will be diagnosed as having alcohol or substance abuse disorders sometime during their lives. All too often, the unfortunate patient who does not respond to incorrect treatment is given the wastebasket diagnosis of "personality disorder" or told he is using his depression as a tool to manipulate others. Aggressive, oppositional and violent teenagers often suffer from an undiagnosed underlying bipolar disorder. Proper diagnosis and treatment is much more effective than weeks or even months of expensive hospitalization.

My interest in this topic developed when, early in my practice, I noticed a significant number of depressed patients who would not respond well to antidepressant medication. They looked improved at first, but, as time went on, they would develop increasing irritability and depression. Increasing the dose of antidepressant did not help, even though that was the common wisdom of how to treat "resistant" patients. Finally, I consulted with a friend and colleague who had done a considerable amount of research into this area. He referred me to articles appearing in mainstream psychiatric journals which described the new information available concerning the concept of mood cycling, or what is more formally known as bipolar type of depression. Once I started paying attention to this area of interest, it became increasingly apparent that I had been missing a very important concept in understanding and treating common depressions. The numerous articles describing the wide variety of bipolar depressions were easily available. It didn't require a great deal of research to become fully informed on the subject. Articles were appearing even in the free journals that most psychiatrists receive routinely, and throw away unread.

Despite the large amount of new information becoming available, I found that my colleagues ignored it. Non-medical professionals with whom I worked did not have easy access to the medically oriented journal articles. When patients were referred to me because they were not responding well to treatment, a careful history would often reveal the patient suffered from some variation of a bipolar disorder. When the referring clinicians were told about this, they would often respond with disbelief and occasionally annoyance. Sometimes, fellow physicians would reverse the treatment I had started, based on the fact that they believed that "no way is this patient manic depressive." The belief was based on outdated concepts of manic depression and bipolar disorders. Patients would generally relapse and return to their state of irritated and agitated depression once the appropriate treatment had been discontinued. Other colleagues became angry at me believing that "you think everybody is manic depressive." As it turned out, a lot of patients sent to me on a referral basis were indeed undiagnosed bipolar patients. This was most likely due to the fact that they were not treated or diagnosed properly in the first place and thus doing poorly.

Eventually, I developed a series of lectures which were originally intended to educate other medical professionals. Surprisingly, this led to fellow physicians wanting to refer their own family members to me since they realized they have suffered needlessly for a long time because of poor diagnosis and treatment. Ultimately, a series of lectures on "Why Your Depression Isn't Getting Better" became very well received and audience members lined up to ask for further information on the more subtle forms of bipolar disorders. Although there were some isolated chapters in various books on depression, there were no books available which specifically dealt with how undiagnosed bipolar depression significantly affects people's lives and ability to function.

Originally, this work was designed to provide information for my personal patients. However, as more and more individuals were seeking information on the topic of bipolar depressions, it became apparent there was a gap in the information base available to the ordinary reader. The purpose of this book is to fill that gap in an entertaining yet informative way.

Chapter One

"I'm Not Manic Depressive"

Jane said she had been feeling depressed for the last year or two. There had been a lot of problems in her life, some marital relationship problems and stress on the job. It seemed like a fairly clear cut case of depression that could be treatable with antidepressants and talk therapy. She was not sure if antidepressants helped or not, and sometimes they made her dizzy or irritable. On further questioning she was able to recall that she had some problems with depression going back to her mid-teen years. She never thought much about it, it just seemed that everybody has periods when they feel down. There were days when she would just pretend to be physically ill and stay home from school. She would draw the drapes and then curl up under the covers, perhaps putting the blanket over her head. Her mother worried about her because during these times she would not come out of her room and eat. Jane explained that she was just feeling ill and she would be alright soon. She would just lie there and think and worry and sometimes cry softly. She would not let her parents see, she was so ashamed. Her moodiness would increase during the premenstrual time of month and she attributed this to her hormones. Her friends told her that hormones do things like this.

Jane eventually was able to get back to school and do fine. There were days when she was even feeling quite well or even better than well. The moods would come and go and then, for periods of time, just seem to even out and she carried on with her life. There were some periods of depression during college. At times the depression would seem so prolonged that Jane considered this just a part of life, simply the way people feel most of the time.

When she was twenty-four years old she had her first child. A few weeks after she gave birth she developed a severe depression during which time she felt suicidal but made no attempts. There was a prolonged period of darkness for her, but she carried on, caring for her youngster as best she could. She finally went to a physician who treated her for the depression with antidepressant medication. She became brighter within a week or two. Jane continued on the medication for the next two or three months and felt very well, so stopped the medication. She seemed to be cured of her problem.

But now, in her thirties, Jane still felt the oppressive weight of depression which sapped energy and spirit. There were some problems to talk about and conflicts to negotiate. But talking about these things did not seem to help all that much right now. Finally, she saw a psychiatrist. She got through the stigma of going to see a "shrink" who prescribed medication, a kind which she had never taken before. It was a new kind of antidepressant. It seemed to help at first but, after a few weeks, the shining effects began to fade and now she felt right back where she started.

When I first saw Jane she looked weary. She sat still in her chair except for her legs which constantly jiggled up and down. "I always do that" she said candidly. "Sometimes I just can't seem to sit still."

I inquired if there was ever any history of bipolar illness or manic depression in her family. "As a matter of fact," she recalled, "there is an aunt on my mother's side who was treated for manic depression. But I know I'm not manic depressive if that's what you're getting at. I've never had any manic episodes." As it turned out, Jane's mother also had problems with serious depression and is responding well to antidepressants even to this day.

"But I'm not manic depressive, if that's what you're getting at." The thought ran through my mind. How many times have I heard that from unsuccessfully treated depressive patients? Her previous treating psychiatrist had the same sentiment. If someone does not have a history of manic episodes, then she cannot be a manic depressive. Could Jane be a manic depressive? Jane didn't think so. Her previous treating psychiatrist did not think so. She had read some books on manic depression and lithium and those books would not seem to point to that diagnosis either. In one sense, they were all correct. Manic depressive illness has some very specific criteria for diagnosis. On the other hand, could this be what is known as a "bipolar" type of depression? And could this explain why she was not responding to standard treatments of depression? An analysis of these questions leads to the unraveling of the mystery of why so many depressions do not respond to what appears to be modern antidepressant therapy.

Throughout the history of psychiatry, the terms "manic depression" and "bipolar" have been used interchangeably, even in scholarly works. It is true that Jane did not have manic depressive illness, but she did have a bipolar disorder. Trying to conceptualize her depression as part of a manic depressive cycle just would not work. So having dismissed the diagnosis of manic depression, her treating physician and psychiatrist also eliminated a whole array of depressions from consideration and this ultimately deprived Jane of proper effective treatment. All that is bipolar is not manic depressive. Manic depression is just one type of bipolar disorder.

The term bipolar refers to having two poles. Just as the earth has a north and south pole or a magnet has a positive and negative pole, bipolar disorders are characterized by a movement between opposite extremes. Manic depression would certainly fit this mold. There seems to be a vacillation between periods of high mood giddiness, euphoria, hyperactivity and low moods of depression, lethargy and tearfulness. But the term bipolar originally used to describe manic depression is somewhat of a misnomer here. Patients like Jane, who have serious problems with depression that come and go, do not move between extreme highs and lows. There are cycles of rising and falling mood, but the mood may never rise to a real euphoric state even though I have heard patients express a desire to experience such a state once in a while. An increase in activity and energy but less than full mania is referred to as hypomania. There are periods of depression and lethargy, but also hypomanic periods of higher energy which may not be perceived as pleasant or desirable. The periods of higher energy may be experienced as an anxiety attack or a period of panic. These anxiety spells may be lengthy, perhaps even chronic. To make matters worse, the periods of increased energy or activation may occur at the same time depression occurs. This is somewhat confusing. It may be hard to perceive of being at opposite poles at the same time. Yet this is just the case with many patients with various forms of bipolar disorder. They are not high and low at the same time, but they are depressed and agitated at the same time. This is known as a mixed state. An agitated depression is more often than not a form of bipolar disorder. During the depressed phase it would be proper to refer to a bipolar depression. As it turned out, Jane suffered from bipolar depression, although technically she was not manic depressive.

There was a long list of clues which helped to lead to the diagnosis of bipolar disorder. Having manic episodes is the least of these clues and may generally be absent altogether. Jane had several signs and symptoms which helped build the case for a proper diagnosis. One of these was the early onset of depression. She started to develop it during her teen years which is very characteristic of this type of depression. She also had a postpartum depression which was quite significant. This was not just the "baby blues" but a serious debilitating problem which kept her from functioning as the wife and mother she wanted to be. There is a family history of serious depression including an actual documented diagnosis of bipolar disorder. There was also her failure to respond to standard antidepressants and to perhaps even get worse with them. All of these clues added up to a very strong suspicion that Jane had a bipolar depression, not the type of depression that would typically respond well to antidepressant medication. There was a strong suspicion, not an absolute certainty. Nonetheless, Jane deserved a trial of a mood stabilizing drug, the type that is used in treating bipolar disorders. Although they are not designed as antidepressants per se, the mood stabilizing drugs do ultimately have some very beneficial antidepressant effect as well as preventing the irritation and agitation or even mania that may develop in the course of a bipolar disorder.

Fortunately for Jane, she responded well to a medication called Depakote. Depakote is one of several medications available for this kind of problem. In the first week of treatment her mood cycling diminished and the agitation became considerably less. The depression persisted, however, and she did require a small dose of standard antidepressant medication. After four months of complying with treatment and combining her medication with ongoing psychotherapy and group support, Jane's moods became stable and predictable and she became more alert and productive.

This may have been some very good news for Jane. The bad news is that she suffered for many years with an incorrect diagnosis and therefore improper treatment. There has never been a more misdiagnosed or misunderstood entity than that of bipolar depression. It is not only the most underdiagnosed and undertreated entity in all of mental health, but probably in all of medicine in general.

The seriousness of this became evident when the first major study of the prevalence of bipolar disorder was published by the American Psychiatric Association in 1993. This study was conducted jointly by the National Depressive and Manic Depressive Association (NDMDA) and the American Psychiatric Association (APA).

This classic study revealed that patients like Jane were the rule more than the exception and that the diagnosis was missed and her treatment was inappropriate.

This study revealed there was a dramatic level of misdiagnosed and delayed diagnosis. On average, the time for correct diagnosis was made eight years after the patient initially sought treatment. Over one third of patients were not correctly diagnosed for more than ten years. Also, on average, patients saw over three doctors before receiving the correct diagnosis.

Although the majority of patients had their first symptoms of bipolar disorder during adolescence, only three percent were actually diagnosed during adolescence.

This study also revealed why proper diagnosis was so important. The treatment for bipolar depression differs from that of other depressions. These data suggest that the incidence of bipolar disorder is much more common than previously thought.

As was the case with Jane, there are frequent relapses in the depression when the patient is treated with antidepressants alone. What also became quite evident is that there is a large amount of drug abuse and alcohol abuse associated with untreated bipolar disorder. A much larger study known as the Epidemiologic Catchment Area study (ECA) included over 25,000 subjects. This massive study sponsored by the National Institute of Mental Health revealed that indeed sixty-one percent of all bipolar patients would, at some time during their lives, have a diagnosable substance abuse disorder. These statistics have very significant implications when we are dealing with diagnosis of alcohol and substance abuse. Many alcoholics are treated for their symptoms of alcohol abuse alone, whereas their underlying mood disorder is ignored or even spurned. Untreated bipolar patients have a tendency to lose their jobs or change jobs frequently.

Dr. Hagop Akiskal , formerly of the National Institute of Mental Health, has done ground breaking research in the area of bipolar disorders, and developed the terms "bipolar spectrum" and "soft bipolar" for the non-manic-depressive bipolar disorders which are often subtle and likewise often missed. He goes on to state that "soft bipolar constitutes a large share of outpatients with affective illness and are often unrecognized and poorly researched and typically mismanaged." He also states that "four to five percent of the population is at risk for developing bipolar spectrum disorder."

Manic depression, which is the original bipolar disorder also known as bipolar I, affects about one percent of the population. Psychiatrists and other mental health professionals would often dismiss the possibility of bipolar depression as being unlikely because of its rarity. Jane has a less dramatic form of bipolar disorder known as bipolar type two.

According to K. Goodwin, M.D., Professor of Psychiatry at George Washington University and senior science advisor to the director of the National Institute of Mental Health, between two and two and a half percent of the population is suffering from bipolar disorder at any given time, which is about twice what was previously thought to be the case. According to Dr. Akiskal's previous estimate, the number of people who actually develop the illness sometime during their life is even higher.

When an illness causes some decreased level of functioning physically or emotionally, it is referred to as "morbidity." The tragedy of bipolar illness is not just the increased amount of pain and life disruption that occurs even when the illness is well treated, but also the extraordinary amount of unnecessary morbidity that occurs because of the massive, epidemic failure of physicians to properly diagnose this type of illness.

The fact is known that bipolar disorder is underdiagnosed and undertreated. It is also known that a significant percentage of Americans suffer with this illness and, at the present time, are being given inadequate or improper treatment. Although this tragedy of unnecessary suffering is clearly documented, the reasons for the failure of health care professionals to make the proper diagnosis has not been studied. You may be one of the millions of Americans and even more millions around the world who have suspected something inadequate about your treatment but, without knowing exactly what the problem is or how to go about correcting it. Although the National Institute of Mental Health, the American Psychiatric Association and the National Depressive and Manic-depressive Association recognize the problem, numerous health care practitioners not only ignore the problem, but are even overtly hostile to the concept of a wide spread untreated bipolar depression.

In this book we will explore the bipolar spectrum and how it affects people's lives in previously unrecognized ways, how it is treated, mistreated, and properly diagnosed.

It is hoped that this knowledge will bring power to the patient and healer alike.

Chapter Two

Why Your Depression Isn't Being Diagnosed

Most antidepressant medications are prescribed by non-psychiatric physicians such as general practitioners, family practitioners and gynecologists. Antidepressant medications and tranquilizers are also widely prescribed by specialists, surgeons, gastroenterologists and internists for a variety of ailments associated with depression and anxiety. A lot of patients who are having problems with depression may not identify it as such and will find their way into the office of their primary care physician. Antidepressant prescriptions are often written for complaints such as lack of sleep or loss of concentration. Unfortunately, there is still a significant stigma attached to treatment for psychiatric disorders. The patient does not want to hear about a diagnosis of depression, nor does the physician want to give it. There can be an unspoken collusion between them.

Surgical and trauma patients in hospitals are often prescribed antidepressants without being told they are being given an antidepressant, but offered the explanation that this is a medication that will reduce the pain or promote sleep. By law, patients on psychiatric wards must sign informed consents for all their psychiatric medications, including antidepressants. On non-psychiatric wards, however, this is not the case, even if the medications are psychiatric in nature. Thus, many patients are being treated for various levels of depression by physicians who do not specialize in this area.

It has been estimated that perhaps eighty percent of patients who show up in a general physician's office have some type of psychological overlay to their primary complaint. This includes complaints in which psychological factors are the primary focus of the illness. In the late 1960s, medical training took a more humanistic approach and there was an increasing focus on treating the patient as a whole being rather than a sum total of anatomical parts and physiologic processes. We started to pay more attention to the dynamics of the patient's home life, lifestyle and belief systems. This was a healthy and humane response of the medical profession to the rapid medical technical advances of the mid-twentieth century.

As technology advanced rapidly, patients felt more isolated and alienated from the medical professionals who were becoming technical in their approach. Patients longed for the caring concerned father figure who was so familiar to families of generations past. Of course, with the new technologies, the physician could actually do more interventions, whereas the forebearers of our profession sometimes had little to do other than to be reassuring, calm and empathetic.

Although psychiatry is a specialty of medicine and is practiced by physicians, the practice of psychiatry was not changing as dramatically as other branches of medicine and surgery.

The specialty of family practice developed in the 1960s and early 1970s. This specialty was unique in that it essentially offered specialized training to physicians who wanted to be general practitioners but more skilled in the various aspects of general medicine. Psychiatry became an important area of education for family practitioners who spent time training in psychiatry units. There was an emphasis on listening and understanding as well as the more scientific and technological aspects of medicine. The idea was to produce a new physician technically skilled but also humane and caring.

Although being humane and caring are desirable and even essential qualities of good physicians (including psychiatrists), these are not sufficient qualities to overcome lack of psychiatric diagnostic skills.

Nonetheless, it became commonplace for non-psychiatric physicians, especially family practitioners and general practitioners, to believe with their training they would have sufficient skill to provide most psychiatric care. Good bedside manner is a wonderful adjunct but not a substitute for psychiatric skills.

One family practice resident once explained to me that he had the psychiatric business pretty well mastered. It seemed straight forward to him that, if the patient is depressed, you give him an antidepressant; if he is anxious, you give him an anti-anxiety agent; if he is psychotic, you give him antipsychotic. What else do you need to know? Another physician, an internist, once explained to me he never refers to psychiatrists because it is basically unnecessary. When the patient becomes nervous, agitated or upset, he just holds her hand and talks to her and sooner or later everything is alright.

Other than lithium, there were few significant advances in psychiatric medication from the 1950s to the late 1980s. Likewise, there were few advances in the art and science of psychiatric diagnosis. It was not hard for a non-psychiatrist to keep up with the latest psychiatric pharmacology. The philosophy of the family practice resident mentioned here seemed to prevail over the years. That is, the patient is depressed, you give him an antidepressant. The bias against psychiatry was no more prevalent anywhere than in the medical profession itself. By and large, general physicians do not have the time or the skills to make definitive psychiatric diagnoses including making the diagnosis of various subtypes of depressions. They see depression as depression, whether it is bipolar, unipolar, the side effect of medication, the result of substance abuse, or the byproduct of underlying physical ailments.

Not only has there been a stigma against psychiatric patients but also against psychiatric practitioners. Some of this prejudice is based on ignorance, but unfortunately some of this stigma has been richly deserved as well.

From the late nineteenth century through the middle and well into the second half of the twentieth century, the basis of psychiatric treatment was not so much medication, but psychotherapy based on psychoanalytical principles. In the late nineteenth and early twentieth centuries, Sigmund Freud wrote many volumes on psychoanalytic theory. His inner circle of followers and disciples learned from him and spread his teachings throughout the western civilized world. The psychiatric establishment operated on the principles of Freud's psychoanalytic theories. Basically, these theories were based on the concept of unconscious motivations which had their roots in the experiences of human growth and development, especially from the perceptions and experiences of infancy and early childhood. Freud went on to propose that depression, anxiety or even psychosis is a result of unresolved unconscious conflicts that derive from experiences in earlier life. By analyzing the occurrences and conflicts in one's earlier life, the unconscious would become conscious and that which becomes conscious can be dealt with. As a result, conflicts could be resolved and anxiety and depression can be cured. Freud's contributions were significant in that he was the first physician to propose that human suffering, both mental and physical, could be explained by evaluating social and family interactions. He also created a therapeutic process whereby talking, expressing feelings and being heard could have curative powers. On the other hand, his theories were just that, theories. Freud came up with brilliant ideas worthy of consideration. However, many of his conclusions were based on non-scientific anecdotal evidence. Still, his work laid the groundwork for modern psychotherapy including the concepts of the unconscious, transference, regression and defense mechanisms.

Until about a generation ago the mainstay of psychiatric training was understanding psychoanalytic theory and its application to psychotherapy. Depression was to be understood in terms of unconscious conflicts, learned about through dream interpretation, free association and conscious childhood recollections. Schizophrenia and manic depression were understood to be a result of dysfunctional interpersonal relationships, particularly in early life and most specifically between that of the mother and the young child.

With the advent of antipsychotic drugs in the early 1950s, little changed in psychiatric theory, even though it was becoming apparent that there were neurochemical processes involved in schizophrenia. In the world of psychiatry, little changed between 1890 and the mid 1950s. Even though the world of medicine was rapidly advancing with increasing knowledge of geometric proportions, the psychiatric practitioner who read his last journal article in 1955 would still be practicing state of the art of psychiatry in the early 1980s. The only significant advance during that period was the introduction of lithium.

This is not to say there were not changes in psychotherapeutic techniques developing. In the 1950s and 60s there was the birth of behavior modification based on the works of pioneers like B. F. Skinner and Joseph Wolpe. During this time there were also the popular works of Eric Berne who popularized transactional analysis which became a trendy but useful therapy in the 1960s and 70s. Fritz Perls introduced Gestalt therapy with its direct confrontive approaches. Also during this time, there was the development of other techniques including cognitive therapy which was a much more pragmatic approach to solving personal problems which provides another basis for today's modern psychotherapy. Despite these developing approaches, Freudian based psychoanalytic therapy remained the most accepted form of treatment for dealing with all types of psychiatric conditions including depression.

Psychiatrists who started to use medications and saw the dramatic results that could often be achieved referred to themselves as "biologic psychiatrists." The term biologic referred to the fact that they were altering biology to a certain extent by using pharmacotherapeutic agents. The effectiveness of the antipsychotic and antidepressant medications was beyond argument. Of course, if medications could alter the course of psychiatric conditions, then certainly one would have to argue that aberrant behaviors and psychosis were more than simply the result of interpersonal interactions that were less than ideal, especially during childhood. Psychiatry entered the age of the medical model.

The medical model implies that a psychiatrist is a "doctor" who treats "patients" and provides diagnoses and treatments. Such concepts were foreign to many psychotherapists who rejected the concept of labels used to describe the various syndromes that psychiatric patients might suffer. Also, consider that the bulk of patients seeing private psychiatrists were not treating truly psychotic patients but often providing counseling for people dealing with various phases of life problems. Such patients have often been sarcastically referred to as the "worried well."

Since biologic treatments were proven to be effective, what would that say about the value of psychotherapy? Over the past quarter century there has been a trend of outcome studies which basically support the notion that psychotherapy alone is useful. The consensus is that psychotherapy is as effective as medications for properly selected patients. It has also been shown that, for many patients, the combination of biologic therapies plus psychological therapies is more effective than either alone.

The use of medications became more widespread, especially with the development of community mental health centers in the 1960s. It was during this time that psychotherapy was becoming no longer the exclusive turf of physicians but was being practiced by nonphysicians. Initially, this meant psychologists with doctorates, but over the last two decades there has been a geometric increase in the number of licensed social workers and the masters level therapists who provide psychotherapy and counseling. This is certainly effective for agencies and other treatment facilities who have to pay much higher hourly rates for physician time than for the nonphysician therapist time. Psychiatrists found themselves moving away from the "shrink" role into more of a medical role of prescribing drugs.. I have even heard the denigrating description of the psychiatrist at the mental health agency as a warm body who can write prescriptions. The social workers and other therapists who are evaluating patients have not been trained in the medical model and utilize an ideologic frame of reference which is often at odds with the medical model. Patients are viewed as a sum total of their psychological and social experiences with perhaps some acknowledgment of biological and genetic parameters.

What has developed over the years is a model where the primary evaluation and therapeutic work is done by a non-physician while a psychiatrist sits in a back room, seeing patients for fifteen minute slots of time writing prescriptions. The concept of careful diagnostic considerations is traditionally alien to the non-physician mental health professionals. The careful teasing out of diagnostic clues is not considered important for a number of reasons. One is that most non-medical practitioners are not trained in medical model approaches. The second is that philosophically, many practitioners do not accept the medical mode preferring to look at current presentations in terms of social and psychological dynamics. It is more the rule than the exception to see an evaluation of a patient with agitated depression based entirely on situational and interpersonal problems. Unfortunately, many physicians will do this as well. This is not to say that situational factors are not important because they are. But to ignore the underlying, physiology and chemistry does an enormous amount of harm to the patient, and leads to continued disrespect for the mental health professions.

Proper treatment of an individual suffering with depression requires proper diagnosis. This involves not only an understanding of the issues and conflicts in his life, but also a carefully detailed history which will explore the quality and nature of symptoms, age of onset, circumstances, and medical and family history. When medications become part of the treatment, it is important for the physician and therapist to communicate as members of a treatment team, which, of course, will involve the patient as well. Treatment will be a multidimensional enterprise of therapy, proper medication when needed, and other elements of lifestyle, blending in a way to make the broken person whole again.

Chapter Three

Alcoholism and Substance Abuse; The Bipolar Connection

Alcoholism and Bipolar Disorder

Similarities

Alcoholism	Bipolar Disorder
0. Excessive use of alcohol	0. Excessive use of alcohol
1. Misses work frequently	1. Misses work frequently
2. Changes jobs frequently	2. Changes jobs frequently
3. Chaotic relationships	3. Chaotic relationships
4. Disturbed sleep pattern	4. Disturbed sleep pattern
5. Poor personal hygiene	5. Poor personal hygiene
6. Impaired judgment	6. Impaired judgment
7. Sobriety essential for treatment	7. Sobriety essential for treatment
0. Family history of alcoholism is likely to be present.	0. Family history of alcoholism is likely to be present.

Alcoholism and Bipolar Disorder

Differences

Alcoholism

1. Usually enjoys or craves alcohol
2. Significant improvement with sobriety
3. No history of mood or sleep cycles
4. Medication not helpful in treatment
5. Can respond well to counseling and support groups

Bipolar Disorder

1. Often does not enjoy alcohol
3. Significant problems persist despite sobriety
4. Strong history of mood and sleep cycles
5. Responds well to lithium and anticonvulsants
6. Needs medication in addition to counseling

Peter is a 41 year old man who was a successful real estate salesman. I first met him when he was accompanied by his wife to the hospital ward. He was a well built, clean cut, good looking gentleman. At first it was not clear why such a successful, well groomed man would be reporting to a psychiatric ward. After he was checked in by the nursing staff, we settled in for our conversation and routine psychiatric evaluation that each patient receives when he arrives in the hospital. He told me he simply was "not able to take it anymore." He had some recurring depressions which seemed to be getting worse. Most recently he had been placed on Prozac, and had been taking this for about four months. At first the Prozac seemed to be helpful in a dose of 20 milligrams daily. This is a very common antidepressant which is well known and frequently prescribed by general physicians. Originally he had not been seen by a psychiatrist but by a family practitioner. It seemed the treatment was working. After a few days Peter was feeling quite well. As a matter of fact, he was feeling better than he had felt in quite some time. Unfortunately, the improvement did not seem to last. Within a few weeks he was feeling more depressed than ever and somewhat agitated as well. His family physician diagnosed him as having an "agitated depression" and felt perhaps what he needed was a higher dose of Prozac. This was moved up to 40 milligrams and, again, an improvement in his mood occurred. Unfortunately, the improvement was temporary once again and he declined into a depression with some increasing irritability. By the time I saw Peter he was on 60 milligrams of Prozac daily and the medication was apparently not effective at all. He complained of feeling temperamental, overwrought and dizzy. He had not been sleeping for the last several nights. It might be easy to go ahead and blame the medication, but a similar type of circumstance occurred about a year and a half ago when he was placed on an entirely different antidepressant from a different class. At that time he had tried a commonly used antidepressant known as Tofranil (or imipramine which is the generic name). He temporarily improved, but the medication rapidly failed him. Larger doses brought only temporary relief followed by irritability, confusion and increasing depression. However, this time the situation was even more serious. Now Peter was contemplating suicide. There had been some stresses going on in his business. The real estate market was on the decline, it was harder and harder to move properties and he had made less income than he had in pervious years. He had been drinking increasing amounts of wine, somewhere between a half bottle and a bottle every evening.

Peter's brother was quite concerned and recommended highly that Peter get help. For the first time in his life Peter saw a psychiatrist who was also alarmed about the suicidal thoughts and recommended that Peter check himself into the hospital. He was somewhat embarrassed about going to a psychiatric hospital but he knew he had to do something. The fact that he was on a high dose of antidepressant and yet feeling more depressed and agitated than ever, and now dwelling on suicide just did not add up. Traditionally, such a depression would be looked upon as an agitated depression and, until this point, that is exactly the way Peter's problem was being treated.

The first and most important intervention that was done for Peter was to stop the antidepressant. This alone can lead to significant improvement in cases such as Peter's. The next most important step was to see that he got a good night's sleep, so a mild sleeping pill was added. He had not been sleeping for several nights and sleeping very little for the nights before that, and this was certainly a very important part of his history. Even though there had been some alcohol abuse, a carefully monitored dose of a sleeping medication under observation in the hospital was considered prudent and necessary. Sleep was an absolutely essential element in Peter's recovery.

Further questioning revealed some very important clues to finding out exactly what was going on here. Peter went through highly productive periods even when the market was not doing well. He was one of the top sellers in the office. But for no reason, his production had started to go down and he was not keeping up with the rest of his colleagues.

Peter had always had a drink from time to time, especially after a hard day selling, but now his drinking was becoming more noticeable. On several occasions he missed morning meetings because he was hung over. At the suggestion of his family physician, Peter started attending alcohol and drug treatment sessions and was started on antidepressant medication, in this case Prozac. For a few weeks the drinking did slow down and he even started to maintain complete sobriety and Peter's mood improved. It did not take long for the moods to cycle even more erratically and for a marked sense of physical agitation to develop. He returned to see his family physician who then referred him to a psychiatric colleague who diagnosed Peter as having agitated depression and increased the Prozac to 40 milligrams a day. The cycle was repeated one more time, whereby Peter's mood improved but his sleep continued to be very poor and he was often pacing. Sometimes he would pop awake at two or three in the morning and would try to read, but he was not able to concentrate. He would take a drink or two to try to get back to sleep. His psychiatrist suggested Peter further increase his medication. However, when he did that he was not able to sit still and attempts at meditating or going through muscle relaxation all proved very unsatisfactory.

Finally, Peter became even more irritable, developing crying spells and outbursts of temper. Although he was normally a prudent driver, he was now speeding more often. Even though he was driving at a fast speed, he made fewer appointments on time. For three days prior to his coming to the hospital he did not show up for work at all and spent his entire nights pacing around or drinking wine so he could get a little sleep, perhaps dozing off for a half hour or so. His thoughts began to increase in rapidity. He felt as if he were in some type of other world. His body began to feel very tense, with tautness throughout his arms and legs and even at times a feeling of anxiety in his gut. Compounding the situation was his feelings of failure as a provider and letting down his family as well as the company for which he worked. Although he wanted to commit himself to sobriety, his mind was racing so rapidly now and his body felt so irritable and tense, he thought alcohol would be the only way he could get some relief. He could drop off to sleep in an intoxicated stupor, but this would be short lived and he would soon awake again with the same feelings of tension and irritability that he tried to escape when he drank.

In an old wooden chest Peter had stored away a hand gun he had purchased about ten years before. He had used it for target practice on a few occasions and fancied that it might provide some good protection. He took out the gun, which was partially disassembled, and started piecing it back together again. He knew he had some bullets somewhere but did not exactly recall where. Ultimately, he held the assembled gun to his hands and stared at it and thought of it as the ultimate way he could finally relieve his agitation and perhaps escape into a more peaceful realm. Fortunately, he knew deep within that this would be something dreadful for him, for his family and for his soul. He called the psychiatrist who was treating him, telling him his symptoms which led to Peter's referral to the hospital.

Even though the referral papers indicated that he was suicidal, he insisted that he actually was not and that he wanted help in getting his life back and begin healing.

After assessing the history and delving for more information, it became apparent that Peter did have periods of depression throughout much of his life. He also had some intermittent periods of excessive energy and could go for long periods of time feeling bright and energetic. No one at the time, least of all Peter, would ever recognize this as the forerunner of what could prove to be a serious and perhaps fatal illness.

As would often be the case with patients like Peter, the failure of an antidepressant would often lead to the trial of a second antidepressant from a different class. It is quite apparent here this was not just a case of simple depression but a case of mood cycling. In analyzing his case history, there were quite a number of factors which would point to the diagnosis of bipolar disorder. The somewhat euphoric energetic "salesman" personality can be sustained for a long time without particular dips in the depression. But more often than that the depression will occur. The development of the racing thoughts and increased drinking are also characteristic. It is quite easy for a mental health practitioner to use the wastebasket diagnosis of "substance abuser" and leave it at that. This also sets up the unfortunate patient to get into some type of battle between the bottle and himself. Certainly the alcohol abuse needs to be addressed but here, as in many cases, it is not the primary problem.

The first intervention was to discontinue the antidepressant and allow him to have a sleeping pill for the first night. He calmed down considerably by the next day, particularly after a good night's sleep of seven hours. Depakote was initiated the next day. In another twenty-four hours Peter reported being considerably calmer. Although maximum benefit from the mood stabilizing drugs may take many weeks, even months, some initial benefits certainly can be noted even after the first dose or two.

Peter became a little more tearful over the next two or three days, but it was not a destructive type of depression he was experiencing. It was merely an honest sadness as he reflected on the issues in his life which had become more prominent in his thinking as the agitation and distractions slowly slipped away. After six days he was ready to leave the hospital. Of course, medication was not the only treatment, but certainly was the keystone in maintaining his ability to be able to function in a reasonably even manner. There was a coordination with the substance abuse treatment center which he agreed to attend on a regular basis to make sure the sobriety remained as part of his ongoing lifestyle. Likewise he needed to reassess his priorities including family, work, recreation and spiritual values and order them in such a way that he had time to live a full, meaningful life which would include time for recreation, spirituality and reflection.

Alcoholism is variously conceptualized as an illness, a moral disorder, a maladaptive behavior, a lifestyle. It has even been defined as a reimbursable disability.

Webster defines alcoholism as "a complex chronic psychological and nutritional disorder associated with excessive and usually compulsive drinking." An alcoholic is, of course, one who engages in or is afflicted with alcoholism.

The excessive use of alcohol has been addressed by our society in a number of ways. The proliferation of alcohol treatment centers, involving both inpatient and outpatient facilities, is related to funding available from insurance companies, county agencies, and the state and federal government to "treat" alcoholism. Large employers often demand alcoholic treatment services as part of the overall health program provided to their employees. Up to $10,000 or more per month can roll in from payors to treatment facilities for one month of treatment for a single patient. Social Security Disability has defined alcoholism and substance abuse as a reimbursable disability. Until recently alcoholics have been considered a protected class under the Americans with Disabilities Act.

It became apparent to me, when I started doing part-time work evaluating Social Security Disabilities claims in the 1980s, that the old aphorism "you get what you pay for" was never truer than when it came to paying people to be disabled. True disability certainly is an issue which any civilized society needs to address. Despite the fact that one could argue that nobody really chooses to be poor and live on the street, it is also true that remuneration for any activity or condition will increase that particular activity. In the world of health care funding, however, it is not the alcoholic who receives the bulk of the financial gain for the existence of such an illness. It is the treatment facilities themselves which can charge very high fees for treatment that also seek to benefit. Often enough, counselors, clinic directors or physicians involved in treating alcoholics are former, or perhaps to use the more politically correct term "recovering" alcoholics. A well publicized case in the mid-1980s involved a clinic director who was fired from his job because, as it turned out, he never really was an alcoholic after all. The difficulty in defining alcoholism derives from the fact that it is indeed a complex subject with many presentations and many causes. It is further clouded by the substantial amount of financial influence that affects the various members of the alcohol treatment community.

At the conclusion of my psychiatric training in the late 1970s, I had the opportunity to visit some luxurious alcohol treatment centers, lovely furniture, great food, low stress atmosphere. I even considered applying for a position in one of these pleasant environments. But if one asks such a question as "is alcoholism really a disease?" as I did, one is likely to get a thoughtful answer but not get hired. To throw open the question of the legitimacy of the disease model of alcoholism is to strike a blow to the gut of the precepts on which alcoholism treatment is based. Of course, if alcoholism is not a disease, no one has much business charging $10,000 a month for psychosocial treatment in a residential setting. In these days of managed care, some of these centers have dried up and have been replaced by more favorable cost efficient outpatient treatment. This may be just as well since there is little or no evidence that residential treatment has any beneficial effect on long term recovery from alcohol abuse. In the alcohol and substance treatment community, many of the strategies used in the approach to the alcoholic patient are based on anecdotes, personal experience and leaps of faith. The approaches to treatment are not based on scientific research or clinical experience.

The American Psychiatric Association study of 1993 and the Epidemiologic Catchment Area (ECA) study from the National Institute of Mental Health both point to strong evidence of a clear association of alcohol and other substance abuse and the various bipolar disorders. The American Psychiatric Association study indicated that forty-one percent of untreated bipolar patients would be experiencing symptoms of a diagnosable substance abuse disorder at any given time. The ECA study published in 1995 and using a much larger data base validated the earlier findings and further revealed that, during the lifetime of a bipolar patient, there was a sixty-one percent probability of a concomitant substance abuse disorder. Basically, this means that the majority of bipolar patients are likely at some time to have a diagnosis of alcohol or some other substance abuse problem.

Does this mean that most alcoholics are bipolar? No one is suggesting that. On the other hand, individuals presenting for treatment of substance abuse should clearly be assessed for the presence or absence of a bipolar disorder. Sitting in a group therapy discussing an individual's battle with the bottle may be helpful for some, but it will not be of much use to the untreated bipolar individual. Various studies have recently started to look at the incidence of undiagnosed bipolar disorder in people presenting for alcohol and substance abuse treatment. More conservative studies suggest that perhaps five to ten percent of all people seeking treatment for substance abuse may have an undiagnosed bipolar disorder and some other studies indicate that this percentage may be considerably higher.

Perhaps the most serious difficulty in defining alcohol abuse and other substance abuses as clear cut disease entities is that this will often fail to recognize the true underlying mood disorder which leads to the alcohol or substance abuse. Unfortunately, there has been a recent trend to separate treatment of alcohol and substance abuse from overall mental health treatment. There are psychiatric hospitals which have separately certified alcohol and substance abuse treatment wards. Employers are demanding treatment for their alcohol and drug abusing employees when they subscribe to a health care plan. Government agencies have been considering alcohol and substance abusers as a protected class of citizens who should not be discriminated against. With these social and financial pressures evident, it is small wonder that clinics, hospitals, and various resorts are being dedicated to the lucrative alcohol and substance abuse business.

Alcohol treatment specialists are generally not physicians and usually have been trained in psychosocial models approaching alcohol abuse. There is great benefit for any given patient learning about alcohol and drug abuse and such knowledge helps the individual deal with whatever affliction he may have. There are physicians who specialize in substance abuse management but they are usually not psychiatrists. The emphasis of these physicians is on the physical effects of alcohol and addictive drugs and what happens during withdrawal and the medical management of dealing with these substances. These physicians are often sequestered in substance abuse treatment facilities. The emphasis in such facilities is generally on "treating alcohol and substance abuse" and not on diagnosis of underlying disorders. This would be similar to treating patients with elevated blood sugars without worrying whether or not they had underlying diabetes.

It may be all well and good for a substance abuse counselor, sleeves rolled up, tie loosened, lecturing to a "client" about knowing alcohol abuse first hand since he has been there and done that and there is no way any alcoholic is going to bs him about how to kick the habit. This approach may be very effective for some, but certainly not for the undiagnosed bipolar patient. There is a great big boat which is being missed. Most nonmedical staff who work with alcoholics and other drug abusers will not recognize the underlying mood cycling and mixed states which drive their clients and patients into the self treatment so common among the undiagnosed bipolar patients.

Treatment is destined to fail with these individuals. The irritability and mixed states continue and are made even worse by attempts at self treatment with street drugs and alcohol. As the situation tends to worsen, the patient is demoted to the category of "problem patient," that is, one who is uncooperative, resistant, and probably with some type of personality disorder.

To worsen matters, many traditional drug and alcohol treatment programs express disdain for medical treatment for underlying disorders. Even when prescribed by a physician, medications are dismissed as "happy pills" or "drugs to solve your problems."

The term "substance abuse" may not be entirely accurate for the self treating individual. Unlike a true alcoholic who gets hooked after using just for the pleasure of it, the bipolar patient may be said to be involved with "substance misuse." He is trying to use the wrong substance to get the right response. Alcohol, which suppresses brain functioning, may take the edge off a mixed bipolar state. It may provide the only pathway to any semblance of sleep. Amphetamine or cocaine may be perceived as maintaining a state of well being and energy, or preventing the physical and emotional collapse which will certainly occur. Often, the self treating, undiagnosed bipolar will say that he really does not like the drugs, but it is the only way he can function.

Unfortunately, excessive alcohol or drug consumption takes on a life of its own, and the individual becomes as addicted as any abuser. When she shows up for treatment, no distinction will be made as to the underlying causes, despite the fact that a little careful history taking will help channel her to the right treatment. Otherwise, she will end up shunted to a drug and alcohol treatment program which will incorrectly teach her that her problems are the cause, not the result of her condition.

Of course, abstinence from addicting substances will be key in treatment since alcohol and drugs will mask the true nature of the underlying disorder, and ultimately compound the problem. Even if proper evaluation and diagnosis is performed, and medical treatment initiated, continuing substance misuse will cause treatment to fail. Bipolar patients will require a combination of approaches which will include substance misuse counseling, proper ongoing medication and monitoring, and therapy which will help with problem solving, education and support.

There has been some interesting research which has pointed to the relationship of genes, family history and alcoholism. Alcoholism does tend to have a familial trend. It has been reported that an alcoholism gene may have been identified. On the other hand, there is strong evidence for a genetic connection in the inheritance of bipolar disorder. The alcoholic genetic factor is theorized to involve faulty metabolism of alcohol. A family history of alcoholism or substance abuse is a supporting factor in making a diagnosis of bipolar disorder. The majority of bipolar patients have a history of alcoholism or substance abuse. More research is needed in this area, but it is clear that there is a strong relationship between bipolar disorders and substance misuse, and this must be explored with every patient/client who walks through the doors of our treatment centers.

Chapter Four

Adolescents and Bipolar Disorder

Jason is a sixteen year old high school junior whose grades have been slipping over the last semester. When he was a sophomore, his grades were in the B range, but lately they have been more like Cs with even a few Ds. He seems to be well behaved, but recently his parents discovered him smoking marijuana in his room. A search of his room revealed a significant amount of smoking paraphernalia including papers, a small bong, a roach clip and less than one half ounce of marijuana in a plastic sandwich bag. His parents were justifiably alarmed and arranged for him to see a private psychiatrist.

Jason revealed that he was feeling angry much of the time and was quite irritable, getting into more and more fights with his parents. He said the marijuana helped calm him down and feel more "in control." A lot of the time he was feeling just plain depressed and said the marijuana helped lift him out of this depression. At times he did not go to school and did not want to tell his parents. Instead, he would wander downtown, in and out of stores, only wishing he could go home and go to bed. Sometimes his sleep was quite poor and at other times he would just lie in bed all day.

Jason's father told him if he would only sleep at night he would not feel so sleepy during the day.

When Jason was alone with his therapist, he sometimes confided that he just could not stand his parents. He did not give a very good reason other than that they were so "bossy" and "authoritarian." He was not eating well and was losing some weight. College was in the family plans, but now Jason was indicating he really did not have an interest in following through with college. Jason's therapist sent him to a psychiatrist who evaluated him as having major depression. He was started on a low dose of antidepressant which did not seem to do any good. Jason's psychiatrist explained to his parents that often antidepressants did not do much good for adolescents but that it was always worth a try.

After a few weeks Jason was placed on a higher dose. The antidepressant never seemed to take hold. He sank into a deeper, darker isolation and withdrawal. His parents discovered suicidal poetry in his room in a notebook he had been keeping by his bed. When he found out they had discovered the notebook and read it, he became enraged, furious. He got into loud, vigorous arguments with his parents. Because of his boisterous antagonism he was placed on restriction. Even though he was not supposed to leave the house, he would sometimes sneak out the window in the middle of the night and go to friends' houses where he would sometimes drink or smoke pot.

One day during his therapy session, Jason revealed he had been hoarding his antidepressant medication because it was not working anyhow and he was planning to overdose on it. His therapist was alarmed and told Jason for his own good he had to be hospitalized, even though it was to be against his will.

On the adolescent ward Jason was often found to be angry, irritable and at times quite isolative. He came to the therapy groups only begrudgingly. He felt humiliated having been forced to be admitted to a psychiatric unit. There was some concern initially that, because of the marked and rapid change of personality, Jason might have some form of adolescent schizophrenia. He also complained of significant depression which persisted, even though he was quite agitated and often seen pacing the hallways. There was also some thought that he may have some type of hyperactivity, but there was no basis for this in the history in that there was no real hyperactivity as a younger child.

All antidepressant medication was stopped as the possibility of a type of bipolar disorder was considered. After a careful discussion with his parents about the risks and benefits and side effects, Jason was placed on a small dose of olanzapine(Zyprexa). This is a relatively new medication which helps stabilize mood and reduce confusion. Within about three days he was considerably calmer and much more redirectable on the hospital ward. Within ten days he was considerably calmer, his mood was brightening and the suicidal urges were almost completely gone. He returned to school the next week. Followup six months later revealed his test scores and attendance had considerably improved and he was functioning much as he had prior to the onset of his behavior change. It should be pointed out that I received an angry call from the therapist who had been treating Jason with traditional psychotherapy. She complained that Jason was really acting out some inner conflicts and that, as a doctor, I should not just be "drugging up" kids who come to my office. She further expressed some anger at the fact that we physicians just like to label people and put them in some type of pigeon hole and give them pills so we can quickly get them out of our office or hospitals to please some HMO insurance company. The final barb was "you would have put Tom Sawyer on drugs if he had come to see you." I could only respond to that by telling her that we, as psychiatrists, do not go out on the street looking for kids to put on drugs, and if Tom Sawyer were suicidal or agitated or depression on an ongoing basis, I would do whatever I could to save his life.

The therapist seemed to have some difficulty in accepting that mood cycling disorders are truly a medical illness every bit as much as diabetes or hypertension and can be just as deadly. I explained to her that I did not think the psychotherapy she was doing with Jason was not valuable. As a matter of fact, certain types of psychotherapy can be useful for hypertension and diabetes as well as for a number of illnesses. Our minds and our bodies are one. So when the disease process focuses on our perceptions, emotions and behavior, why should be deny anyone the best treatment available which, as for any illness, would combine the best of medical, psychological and spiritual approaches. That would apply to hypertension, diabetes, asthma, as well as panic attacks, depression or alcoholism. Cardiac disease is never treated exclusively with pills and by the same logic, significant psychiatric illness often cannot be treated with "psychotherapy" alone. The therapist and I made further contacts around Jason's progress. Jason benefitted from our combined efforts and received the best multidimensional treatment we could provide together.

Teenagers probably suffer more than any other group because of the common misdiagnosis and mistreatment of bipolar disorder. One might find this quite curious considering the large amount of financial and human resources allocated to treating teenagers with psychiatric difficulties, particularly those with generous insurance.

Up through the mid to late 1980s it was common for hospitalized teens to actually live in a psychiatric hospital. They would attend school and live on the hospital ward. It would not be unusual for the hospitalization to last six months or perhaps even a year or more.

As a naive psychiatric resident first exposed to the adolescent psychiatry ward, I was curious to find out why kids who seem to be functioning fairly well, looking cheerful, interacting well and appearing to be free of significant psychotic symptoms were continuing in lengthy hospitalization. Explanations were usually vague but generally along the lines of "she's not ready to go home yet" or "there are significant problems with the family." Placement away from a dysfunctional home might be a very good idea for a troubled youth, but it seems there were probably more economical and efficient ways to provide this than living in a facility that would cost eight hundred to a thousand dollars a day. It was a rare occasion that hospitalization was necessitated by a long term unremitting psychotic process.

Many of these kids were initially hospitalized because of bad behaviors, depression, and suicide gestures. Often, away from the stresses of a dysfunctional home life, they would do better.

Psychiatric treatment, especially hospital treatment for adolescents, is steeped in psychosocial models and developmental psychology. Most programs correctly apply structure and limits to behavior. Irritability, outbursts and fighting are not simply bad behavior but are elements of "acting out." The term "acting out," to use the psychoanalytic jargon, implies the external physical aggression of unconscious internal conflicts. In the world of adolescent psychiatry, there are official diagnoses that include Conduct Disorder and Oppositional Defiant Disorder. To qualify for such a diagnosis, the patient must meet several behavioral criteria. Diagnosis, however, does not necessarily imply any underlying cause. These are merely descriptive terms. The case of Jason typically illustrates the story of an individual with mood cycling who was not diagnosed in a timely manner. As has been pointed out, delayed diagnosis in bipolar disorder of all types is more the rule than the exception for adolescents.

We now know that adolescence is the most common time during the life cycle for the symptoms of a bipolar disorder to develop. According to the 1993 study done by the American Psychiatric Association, the teen years are when sixty percent of bipolar patients first experience symptoms. Yet only three percent of bipolar patients are first diagnosed during that time. That is, only one out of twenty bipolar patients is first diagnosed properly during adolescence. The consequences of missed diagnosis are enormous not only because of unnecessary suffering and expense, but also, because the more episodes of bipolar illness anyone suffers, the more difficult it becomes to treat later episodes of the illness and future episodes of illness become more frequent.

Basically, brief inpatient treatment based on accurate evaluation and diagnosis is far superior to what one former teacher of mine called "chronic undifferentiated therapy." There are too many Jasons whose lives are being sidetracked indefinitely because the system which is supposed to help is failing them.

Part of the problem is the psychodynamic and psychoanalytic orientation of the child psychiatrist. To become a certified one must complete a psychiatric residency which already includes some child psychiatry training, then complete an additional one or two year fellowship in child and adolescent psychiatry. The length of the additional training depends somewhat on the structure of the program.

Training in child psychiatry focuses on psychoanalytical models and developmental psychology in general. The psychoanalytic model, based on the works of Sigmund Freud involves the psychological development of a human being from birth starting with the oral stage of development and working up to anal, phallic, latency and Oedipal stages. Freud tied these concepts to the development of the unconscious. In developing a "map" of the unconscious mind, he developed the terms id, ego and superego.

In understanding the development of a child, classic psychiatry holds it essential to understand this model and to apply it to aberrant behaviors which are largely deemed to result from the acting of unconscious conflicts. Other developmental models include the works of Piaget who formed a useful frame of reference in understanding the cognitive development of the child. Erik Erikson's model of the various stages of life describes universal psychological conflicts which shape the interactions of human beings from birth through senility.

The child psychiatrist is also trained in understanding object relations which describes the nature of attachments between the infant and the important people in the environment, especially the mother. Typically, the child/adolescent therapist treats a family or a "system" and not just an individual patient. Very often the teenage patient who has presented for treatment is actually an emissary from a highly dysfunctional family. Learning to treat children and adolescents in the context of their school, family and environment is intellectually challenging, stimulating and often rewarding. It is also the most difficult area of psychiatry because it is so complex.

But with all the thoroughness and intensity of training in this area, the practitioner is often ill prepared to do a diagnostic medical evaluation. It is not surprising, then, that clear cut diagnoses are often missed because the therapist or physician is not approaching the patient using a framework which would support a diagnosis based on history, signs and symptoms. This is not to say that these developmental frameworks are not of use. The concepts advanced by the pioneers in psychology and psychiatry have provided us with enormously useful theories and ideas which enhance our abilities to treat our patients. Yet these concepts have their limitations because, although they address human development and its aberrations, they do not define illness, nor are they supposed to.

Freud developed a system which provides us a frame of reference for understanding human behavior. Although some of his concepts are obsolete, I would like to think that if Freud were alive today, his intense creativity and insight would also focus on diagnostic concepts that are becoming more available to us.

Certainly, not all bad behavior in teenagers is due to bipolar disorder. Kids can be bad actors, spoiled, and subject to evil peer pressures. Many abuse drugs, not for any self treatment purpose, but just because peers do it or because "it feels good." The lack of parental structure in the home due to career demands or divorce is leading to an increasing amount of antisocial behavior in teens. In western culture, adolescence is a time of rebellion and limit testing. Careful analysis and investigation is required to really figure out what is going on with any youngster who shows up for treatment. It is extremely important to differentiate pathologic behaviors in teenagers from age appropriate rowdiness. The evaluator needs a certain degree of real curiosity and a desire to find out what is really going on with the adolescent patient.

Recent studies add further validity to the argument that bipolar disorder is much more common among psychiatrically hospitalized adolescents than previously thought. It has even been suggested that bipolar disorder is the most common diagnostic entity among hospitalized adolescents. The question has also been raised whether conduct disorders should be treated with mood stabilizers. Several studies have shown a strong relationship between conduct disorder and bipolar disorder in adolescents. Confounding the picture is the fact that a lot of children and adolescents with a diagnosis of attention deficit hyperactivity disorder have associated bipolar disorder as well. A number of problems including conduct disorder, attention deficit disorder and substance abuse are strongly associated with bipolar disorder. Adolescence is the primary age for onset of bipolar disorders, and with new information becoming available about the widespread prevalence of this condition we need to take another look at the illnesses that bring adolescents into the psychiatric hospital.

The increasingly large percentage of bipolar patients seen in psychiatric hospitals and emergency rooms is related to the fact that the diagnosis is missed in the first place. Nonbipolar depressed patients who respond well to antidepressants will not need further treatment in the more structured and restrictive environment such as the hospital. The agitated and suicidal patients who make their way to the emergency rooms or hospitals are often the treatment failures of various clinicians. Of course, the reason for many treatment failures is the failure of proper diagnosis in the first place. It naturally follows that the population of patients in crisis is skewed toward a bipolar diagnosis.

One of the disturbing paradoxes in observing younger children on the psychiatric wards is trying to reconcile presentation of a child who is very sweet and endearing throughout much of the day but at other times ends up screaming totally out of control and perhaps becoming even recklessly violent on even the smallest provocation. This is bewildering to hospital staff, parents and even to the children themselves. Indeed, some of these children do come from very disturbed dysfunctional families. Careful evaluation and a diagnostic consideration of a bipolar variant needs to be exercised before the child is relegated to the diagnostic dust bin of having some type of "acting out" disorder and put on a six month regimen (or however long insurance benefits are good for) of structure and confrontation. Even worse would be the misdiagnosis of attention deficit disorder with hyperactivity and placing the child on stimulant medication which may even make the situation worse. Children who don't respond to treatment with stimulants or antidepressents should be evaluated carefully for a bipolar disorder. This could be lifesaving for children, and to some extent, their families as well. Sometimes, a history of uncontrolled explosive outbursts in a child are associated with subtle brain injury during pregnancy or birth. Although this is not due to bipolar disorder, anticonvulsants can be very effective in controlling this behavior. Antidepressants may make the situation worse whereas stimulants such as Ritalin could be effective depending on the nature and extent of the underlying disorder.

Careful evaluation and the application of a little common sense can make a huge difference in the outcome of treatment.

Chapter Five

Hyperactivity and Bipolar Disorder

Hyperactivity and Bipolar Disorder

Similarities

Bipolar	ADHD
1. Rapid mood cycles	1. Rapid mood cycles
2. Impulsiveness	2. Impulsiveness
3. Drug/alcohol abuse	3. Drug/alcohol abuse
4. Attention deficits	4. Attention deficits
5. Motor hyperactivity	5. Motor hyperactivity
6. Difficulty completing tasks	6. Difficulty completing tasks
7. Marital instability	7. Marital instability
8. Hot tempered	8. Hot tempered
9. Vocational instability	9. Vocational instability
10. Hyperverbal	10. Hyperverbal

Hyperactivity and Bipolar Disorder

Differences

Bipolar

1. Sleep cycling
2. Onset adolescence/young adulthood
3. Cycles of days, weeks, months
4. Not associated with learning disabilities
5. Not associated with neurologic signs
6. Sustained drive, activity, c an be productive
7. May have low energy periods
8. Gets more irritable with stimulants
9. Tends to destabilize with antidepressants.
10. Calms with tranquilizers

ADHD

1. Hypersomnia not likely
2. Childhood hyperactivity
3. Very rapid mood changes, instability
4. Associated with dyslexia, other learning disabilities
5. Soft neurologic signs
6. Does not sustain drive long enough to be productive
7. Generally "hyper"
8. Calms with stimulants
9. May stabilize with antidepressants
10. May get more irritable with tranquilizers

In the late 1980s and early 1990s there was a resurgence in the concept of attention deficit hyperactivity disorder particularly as it applies to adults. Some psychiatrists and neurologists started developing practices diagnosing and treating various types of hyperactivity, particularly as this diagnosis applied to adults The diagnosis of minimal brain function (MBD) became a very popular diagnosis in th early 1980s. This caught on as a rather trendy diagnosis for adults, but ultimately faded in significance and popularity as data failed to prove this was a prevalent problem among adults. The tying together of childhood hyperactivity with the minimal brain dysfunction of adults was a natural trend since data were very incomplete regarding the prognosis of hyperactive children as they grow into adolescence and adulthood.

In a May 1994 article in the American Journal of Psychiatry, David Shaffer of Columbia University estimated the prevalence of attention deficit hyperactivity disorder (ADHD) in adults to be about 0.3 percent. The current volume of the Psychiatric Diagnostic Statistical Manual estimates bipolar II disorder to be a lttle higher than that. However, research developing from the National Institute of Mental Health and other sources indicates that the incidence of the bipolar spectrum disorders is considerably higher, perhaps ten times as high as that estimated in the DSM IV. At the same time the DSM IV estimates ADHD in children at a three to five percent prevalence rate, while it is acknowledged that data for this disorder persisting into adulthood are very limited.

Like bipolar disorder, there is a great deal of confusion about diagnosis of ADHD, its possible misdiagnosis and even probable overdiagnosis. The diagnosis of attention deficit hyperactivity disorder in children has long been controversial since there are many social and environmental factors tied up in the clinical presentation of a child who presents with excessive motor activity and mood cycling. In adulthood, there is a profound connection of ADHD to substance abuse disorders, anti-social behaviors and overall difficulty in functioning. Children in the United States tend to be diagnosed as having a hyperactivity syndrome more frequently than their peers in other parts of the world. America has an aggressive acting out culture which translates into short attention span, overall hyperactivity and impulsiveness.

There is a great deal of overlap between the signs and symptoms of rapidly cycling bipolar disorders and the signs and symptoms of a hyperactivity disorder. However, the hyperactivity disorder is not particularly well defined in adults, nor is there much research or literature about this. The minimal brain dysfunction syndrome which is essentially the same as ADHD in adults is not addressed as a diagnostic entity in adults. In America, the attention deficit hyperactivity disorder is a condition diagnosed primarily in children with one of the criteria being an onset of symptoms prior to age seven. Diagnostic criteria include easily distractability, forgetfulness, and difficulty engaging in tasks that require sustained mental effort. Other criteria for diagnosis include being restless, running about excessively, and as stated in the DSM as "often on the go" or "often acts as if driven by a motor." We can see that some of these symptoms look like early bipolar disorder, but of course there are some distinct differences between the syndromes. What looks like hyperactivity syndrome in adults can also closely resemble the mild brain impairment which is often seen with chronic substance abuse. This is what complicated the previously discussed case of Cecil. Although there are adults with true hyperactivity disorder, it is not nearly as common as the bipolar spectrum disorders which are pervasive.

Hyperactivity and manic symptoms may be found with bipolar disorders, drug abuse, drug withdrawal, attention deficit hyperactivity disorder, organic impairments and medical disorders. How is one to know? There is a significant amount of information which suggests the disorders overlap to a considerable degree. It is also true that attention deficit hyperactivity disorder will overlap with substance abuse disorders and the behavioral problems that accompany substance abuse.

Paul Wender, M.D. and his colleagues at the University of Utah have developed a series of criteria for identifying ADHD in adults. Like bipolar disorder, Wender and his colleagues contend that the ADHD is a markedly underdiagnosed and undertreated condition. The confusing element, however, is that many of the symptoms of ADHD are very similar, if not identical, to those described for bipolar disorders in adults. Also, there is a marked overlap of symptoms which could be consistent with personality disorders.

The primary difference between ADHD and bipolar disorder is that attention deficit disorder is a chronic ongoing condition with irritability and impulsiveness whereas it would be more likely that the bipolar individual would have episodic spells. Also, the primary diagnostic criteria for attention deficit hyperactivity disorder are largely based on behavior and not on mood states. The very hyperactive child or even adult tends not to sleep cycle but paradoxically is often able to have a fairly good night's sleep.

It is generally considered that the true deficit hyperactive patient had an onset of symptoms early in childhood with documentable symptoms or perhaps even treatment. Deep, lengthy, low energy depressions would not be characteristic in an individual with attention deficit hyperactivity disorder. Likewise, a patient with attention deficit hyperactivity disorder may have what is known as "soft neurologic signs" such as delays or minor deficits of coordination, speech development or reading development. This is where the concept of "minimal brain dysfunction" comes in. This implies there are not only disturbances in behavior but also of coordination and to some extent certain cognitive and intellectual functions. This is generally not considered to be the case with bipolar disorders.

The various treatments will also help differentiate between the diagnoses. The medications used in the treatment of bipolar disorders are not at high risk for being abused. The exception is the minor tranquilizers, the benzodiazepines such as Ativan, Valium, Klonopin, etc. The treatment for attention deficit hyperactivity disorder would be quite different.

Children are treated with the amphetamine like drug, methylphenidate which is also known as Ritalin. Stimulants tend to paradoxically quiet down the hyperactive child and, by extension, will also quiet down the hyperactive adult. One of the clues in making a diagnosis is that the amphetamine misusing adult will often report feeling calmer after using the medication.

ANN—A Case of Adult Hyperactivity

Ann is a twenty-nine year old woman who has been clean and sober and not using amphetamines for the last two years. She decided she wanted to get straight with her life, become clean and sober and make her relationship with her boyfriend work so they could eventually get married. He did not want to marry her while she was still abusing drugs. She went through a twelve-step program for a while and was able to kick the amphetamine habit. But in the two years since she stopped using the amphetamines, she has gotten more irritable, agitated and combative. On several occasions she had struck her boyfriend during arguments. He had not been physically abusive toward her. She becomes remorseful after this occurs. She finds herself sleeping less and becoming more irritable. Her moods have been cycling more rapidly. She has been able to function at her job as a manager in a retail store, but has been finding it increasingly difficult to get through the day. She will drink several cups of brewed coffee in the morning and finds this calms her somewhat and helps her get through the day. However, in the evening she becomes very irritable and her boyfriend, with whom she had been living, ultimately needed to move out for his own physical safety and self protection. She had been to the psychiatric clinic where she was diagnosed as having depression with possible bipolar disorder. However, she had tried lithium and Depakote, both to no avail. She had also been put on low doses of the major tranquilizer, Stelazine, at one point, and later, Navane, and found these just made her confused. It was felt that perhaps she had an agitated depression and a mild tranquilizer (Ativan) was of very little help and she found that perhaps made her even more agitated.

After some careful questioning, it became clear from her history the amphetamines were used to help calm herself down. Bipolar individuals, on the other and, will classically state they used the amphetamines to get themselves "up" motivated and get through the day and give themselves energy. Such is not the case of the adult who classically has a hyperactivity syndrome. Ann was ultimately placed on a stimulant drug, pemodine (Cylert), and this seemed to be quite helpful. When placed on a therapeutic dose, she found herself calmer, able to rest better and many of her symptoms of irritability and agitation abated.

The difference between Ann and a person who would have been diagnosed as bipolar is in her response to treatment. Sometimes the attempts at treatment really do help clarify the diagnostic issues. Some careful history taking revealed that Ann was restless and disruptive in elementary school and always had difficulty focusing on her work. She was never tested for hyperactivity as a child. We referred her for testing which confirmed that she most likely had ADHD.

At first glance, Ann would appear to be an amphetamine misusing bipolar individual who became dysfunctional after stopping the use of her drug of choice. Obviously, it would be poor form to advise any individual with a mental disorder to go back and start using street drugs to treat their symptoms. There are stimulants available in a pharmaceutical preparation which can prove to be very useful. Some physicians will prescribe Dexadrine which is an amphetamine which is somewhat stronger. The drug Cylert is not particularly abused since it takes several weeks of use to start having a significant effect. Patients who take Cylert do not get the usual "buzz" they get with other types of amphetamine like drugs.

Caffeine is also a stimulant, and very often individuals with attention deficit hyperactivity disorder will state they need to drink large doses of brewed coffee throughout the day in order to keep themselves reasonably calm. Once again, the right questions have to be asked and a very careful history has to be noted in order for the proper diagnosis to be made.

What is the likelihood that an individual adult, adolescent or child has both of these disorders?

Scott West and his team of researchers published a series of studies looking at the possible overlap of attention deficit hyperactivity disorder and bipolar disorder in adolescents. Although study samples were small, there was significant evidence there was indeed overlap in the symptomatology of adolescents hospitalized with acute mania. Meticulous history taking revealed that the attention deficit hyperactivity disorder symptoms predated the onset of the bipolar disorder by over five years. Other co-morbid disorders, not surprisingly, include substance abuse and anxiety disorders. Likewise, it was found that adolescents who had the attention deficit hyperactivity disorder component tended to be male.

Looking at it from the other direction, Joseph Biederman in a 1996 study from Massachusetts General Hospital, found a significant percentage of 140 patients diagnosed with attention deficit hyperactivity disorder had or developed bipolar disorders. It was also his contention that, although attention deficit hypeactivity disorder and bipolar disorders are often confused, they are separate and distinct entities. His conclusion was that children with attention deficit hyperactivity disorder are at an increased risk of developing bipolar disorder. This leads to some specific treatment problems. The specific pharmacologic intervention for one disorder may worsen the other. For example, given a tranquilizer to a hyperactive child may actually make the hyperactivity worse. Giving a stimulant to an individual with bipolar disorder will more than likely cause agitation, irritability and decompensation. And what about the long term drug abuser who may have one or both of these disorders underlying his behavioral and mood problems? Furthermore, how can we be sure what the exact diagnosis or mix of diagnosis really is? There are diagnostic criteria from the Diagnostic and Statistical Manual and also various scales to identify and quantify various types of behavior. Fortunately, very careful analysis of a patient's symptoms, not only in the present time frame but over the longitudinal course of the patient's history, can help clarify the situation and lead to the effective treatment and reduction of symptoms in most cases.

One important historical clue is the presence of learning disabilities such as dyslexia which involves difficulty in properly reading and interpreting written language. Other disabilities which involve receiving information or being able to express it properly either verbally or through written communication, are closely associated with attention deficit hyperactivity disorder. These are problems which stay with the child through adolescence and into adulthood, although a highly motivated adult can certainly learn to overcome these disabilities to some extent. The adolescent who develops mood cycling, irritability, and diminished functioning in school and perhaps at home is more likely to be suffering from a mood disorder which would include a significant probability of an early bipolar disorder.

Age fifteen to nineteen is the most common window for developing early bipolar symptoms. The finding of academic slowdown or even failure that develops in later adolescence would not be particularly consistent with attention deficit hyperactivity disorder since it is much more closely associated with disabilities or symptoms that develop in early childhood, perhaps even from birth. Likewise, drug abuse history has to be very carefully assessed. As has been pointed out, drug abuse, either current or historical, can very much confound the clinical picture and one cannot always be certain the patient is telling the truth about drug history.

It is quite routine to perform at least a urine drug screen on any mood disordered patient who is requiring hospitalization. It is not surprising to see even the most adamant deniers of drug abuse turn up positive for amphetamines, cocaine, marijuana, alcohol or other substances. Even when confronted, patients will often minimize the finding by acknowledging that perhaps they were doing some drugs just this past week "just once or twice" and "I just forgot about it."

Psychiatric diagnoses are not magical in such complex cases. If an adolescent or adult is developing mood cycling and hyperactive symptoms, certainly the diagnosis of bipolar disorder should be looked at first. If there is a long history of problems going back to early childhood with problems involving ability to function in school in the early grades, then the attention deficit hyperactivity disorder diagnosis should be considered instead of or in addition to a bipolar diagnosis.

So the next question would be how to manage disorders when there is a combination of problems. Treatment of one might cause worsening of another! The physician must first look at treatments that would lead to the most likelihood of benefit and the least likelihood of harm. Sometimes the response to treatment itself will be a good clue for further directions in what medications to use and which programs to attend. The diagnosis of ADHD implies a life long disturbance in neurobiologic functioning. There may be electroencephalogram abnormalities and the disturbances noted on the brain imaging studies particularly positron emission tomography (PET scans). The PET scan holds excellent promise for assisting in diagnosis of various psychiatric syndromes.

Because of the overlap of ADHD and its predisposition to be associated with bipolar disorder, the key to understanding and treating such disorders lies not in the advanced technology which is becoming available, but in the plain old fashioned hard work of history taking, gathering information, putting clues together and solving the riddle which comes before us.

Chapter Six

Dueling Diagnoses

Cecil explained that his life had become a hell of up and down moods, irritation, flights of temper and poor performance at work. He was not sleeping even with prescribed sleeping pills. He had a history of moodswings going back to his early teens. There were periods of depression and times of excitement and irritability. As a child, his teachers thought he might be hyperactive although he was never formally tested.

During this interview he and his wife appeared quite devoted to each other, but after the evaluation his wife confided she was really afraid of him, even though she loved him. She could not go on living the way she had been living and would consider leaving him. This was quite a bind for her since Cecil kept insisting he would kill himself if his wife ever left him.

After being in the hospital for only a day or two, Cecil seemed to be very cheerful, outgoing and leading the group discussions. There was no more talk of suicide. He did not look like somebody who needed to be in the hospital. With this type of history, though, it appeared he would need to be on some sort of medication to stabilize his mood. He had been on numerous antidepressants, all of which had failed. This meant they caused him to get very agitated, sleepy, confused or more irritated. Large doses of sleeping pills were not getting him to sleep. Finally, another physician had prescribed lithium and this seemed to calm him down, but after a while the lithium did not seem to be very effective either.

Cecil had been a heavy amphetamine abuser, but now he had been abstaining and clean for the last two and a half years. He had gotten hooked on it since it was cheap and easily available in the area where he lived. He started abusing drugs during his teen years because they either calmed him down or prevented depression from coming back, at least temporarily.

With the information available so far, there were numerous considerations as to the real nature of the problem. Was there a bipolar disorder? Could this be attention deficit hyperactivity disorder?(ADHD)or a combination of both? And just how did all the drug abuse play into this?

It is well known that frequent use of amphetamines causes some significant changes in the structure and function of his brain. Another good question was why was he having so many problems two and a half years after discontinuing use. Part of that answer is that he really was still abusing drugs and not telling anybody. The amphetamines were not really calming him but making him feel more energetic. It was clear that this usage caused his mood to destabilize and lead him to become more tense and argumentative. He had developed a true addiction. This made his underlying psychiatric problems even more unstable and resistant to treatment.

During the acute phases of amphetamine intoxication, one can look just as if he has schizophrenia or perhaps a manic illness. Amphetamines stimulate dopamine receptors in the brain excessively just as it is suspected these same dopamine receptors are sensitive to excessive simulation in schizophrenia or perhaps manic episodes. Dopamine is one of many transmitters in the brain, but one of the most prominent and best studied. Since it is involved in the perception of pleasure, it is intimately involved in addiction.

Amphetamine abuse or intoxication has been considered to be a model for the understanding of psychosis. Continued stimulation of nerve cells in an abnormal way can change their form and function over time. The drug, in essence, is a toxic substance and, when used in excess, can have permanent damaging effects.

Most of us are familiar with the concept of a "burned out sixties hippie." The burned out metaphor can also be used with the concept of a chronic amphetamine abuser or "speed freak." Perhaps while no longer abusing drugs the individual will remain eccentric, perhaps somewhat paranoid and often unpredictable.

This brings us back to our patient Cecil who was continuing to fail at various attempts at treatment. Cecil would often get cantankerous, or perhaps euphoric, sometimes suicidally depressed, even while on massive doses of medication. At times, he certainly looked as though he were manic. Yet it seemed no amount of medication would get him to sleep for the night, but at other times he would tend to sleep excessively. How much of this was due to bipolar illness or ADHD would be almost impossible to determine now. What is clear is that Cecil had some type of residual brain damage leading to his lack of behavioral control.

Patients like Cecil are singularly difficult to treat. Not only does he have an underlying psychiatric illness, but the structure and function if the brain has changed, making him resistant to the usual medication treatments. Although it is clear from his history that he has some type of emotional instability, the alcohol and substance abuse distort the picture. Over time, and with true abstinence from illegal drugs, an individual can calm down, although there may be certain permanent losses in the ability to focus and concentrate. At least the violence and irritability might come under control. Sedating medications, antipsychotics and mood stabilizers may offer some relief, but the response is not really predictable.

Over the next six months Cecil was hospitalized five or six times. He voluntarily entered the hospital in some type of suicidal crisis only to become calmer or more cheery within the next few days and checked himself out. He was never able to return to work. He recognized that he needed to find an environment where drugs would not be so readily available and moved away to a more rural area where he would have the support of his family of origin. After numerous trials of medications, he ultimately seemed to do the best on no medications whatsoever as long as this meant not taking any illegal drugs as well.

Amphetamines and other stimulants are the favorite drugs of choice for bipolar and ADHD patients. As can be expected, the use of such drugs will have a marked destabilizing effect. An individual with a tendency toward mania or hypomania who self treats with drugs such as amphetamines or marijuana, will generally experience many severe psychotic episodes and a gradual overall deterioration of ability to function. He runs a very high risk of spending the rest of his life on the disability roles, and becoming a non-productive member of society. In this respect, the drug and alcohol counselors are absolutely correct. That is, without abstinence there can be no treatment.

Unstable moods are not just the result of bipolar illness. They can also arise from ongoing use of such substances as amphetamines, cocaine or even excessive caffeine. Adults with ADHD also can look manic as well. Brain injury can result from physical trauma such as a fall or from use and of abuse recreational drugs and this can lead to hyperactive, manic-like episodes as well. Treatment certainly needs to go beyond the proper selection of medications. The patient will need to remain in a structured and supportive environment with ongoing counseling including treatment around the substance abuse and continuing abstinence.

The concept of dual diagnosis is perhaps the first step whereby alcohol and substance abuse programs acknowledge coexisting psychiatric disorders. It is only a very rudimentary first step, however, since the term dual diagnosis implies that the patient has alcohol and substance abuse and some other psychiatric disorder, but does not imply that they are really related or both manifestations of the same problem. So now specialized dual diagnosis therapy groups have been established. It is as if "flash, stop the presses!" psychiatric patients, particularly those with mood disorders, also frequently have alcohol and drug abuse problems.

We know that adults with ADHD and bipolar disorders abuse alcohol and drugs at a significantly higher rate than the general population. These are conditions which generally respond to treatment, so it is a big mistake to ignore them and just focus on substance abuse treatment. The majority of bipolar patients , at some time in their lives, has diagnosable alcohol or substance abuse. It has also been shown that hyperactive adults are much more likely to be involved in substance abuse. We also are beginning to understand that many of these bipolar patients use the substances to self treat their symptoms and thereby "misuse" and not "abuse" the substances. When this happens, it is practically impossible to figure out how much of the problem causes substance abuse, and how much was caused by substance abuse. When it comes to these disorders, however, we know they go together.

Perhaps these programs will evolve to the point whereby the concept of substance abuse treatment will be, at some level, distinguished from substance misuse treatment. The result would lead to a more effective total approach to treatment and not just focus on abuse problems.

Chapter Seven

South of the Borderline

Borderline and Bipolar

Similarities

Borderline	Bipolar
1. Emotional instability	1. Emotional instability
2. Alcohol and substance abuse	2. Alcohol and substance abuse
3. Impulsive behavior	3. Impulsive behavior
4. Chaotic relationships	4. Chaotic relationships
5. Suicidal behaviors	5. Suicidal behaviors
6. Temper outbursts	6. Temper outbursts
7. Periods of high functioning	7. Periods of high functioning

Borderline and Bipolar

Differences

Borderline

1. Superficial self cutting
2. Symptoms more chronic and sustained
3. Feelings of emptiness and boredom
4. Clingy, needy in relationships

5. Frequently a history of abuse or molestation
6. Poor self esteem
7. "Splitting"

Bipolar

1. More serious suicide attempts
2. Symptoms episodic

3. Keeps busy
4. May be irritable, pulls away in a relationship
5. Family history of depression, substance abuse
6. May have inflated ego
7. Relates in more consistent manner

Personality disorders are referred to in the diagnostic and statistical manual (DSM IV) as a mental condition. The diagnosis of the various types of personality disorder have been developed over the years so that when mental health professionals speak to each other, there will be a common understood meaning of what is being discussed. Also, if there is no diagnosis to put on the insurance form, there won't be any payment.

Personality disorder diagnoses are also very useful if we, as professionals, are not really sure what the diagnosis is, we can assign some type of label that will make everyone feel that the unclear has been clarified.

Perhaps the most insulting label in all of psychiatry is being referred to as "borderline." Over the years there have been numerous articles written and many conferences given on the topic of medicating the borderline patient. At times it seems like practically any type of medication is recommended and practically none of them work.

The diagnostic term borderline personality disorders involves specific criteria to make the diagnosis. As it turns out though there are many individuals who carry the diagnosis based not only on their own behavior but also on the frustration of the practitioner trying to make the diagnosis. Unfortunately, many undiagnosed bipolar patients get dumped into this category. The result is a preconceived notion of what is wrong and no further significant diagnostic inquiry is taken. In psychiatry in particular, once a diagnosis is assigned, it can stay with the patient for a mighty long time. The diagnosis is made much more commonly in females than males. There are basically two clusters of traits in the diagnostic manual, one of which involves the irritable and agitated behaviors. The other cluster involves a sense of emptiness, loneliness and neediness. This second cluster of traits is not particularly associated with bipolar disorder. One disturbing behavior which is quite characteristic of the borderline patient but not of the bipolar patient is the tendency to inflict injury on oneself such as cutting oneself, usually superficially. Often the patient will say this doesn't hurt, but on the contrary, tends to relieve their sense of irritation.

The classic borderline personality has been described by the psychoanalytic writer Helene Deutsch. She described a personality so devoid of a sense of self, that she takes on the characteristics of those around her. She gets in a suffocating relationship with a man and incorporates his qualities and characteristics as her own. She has no identity other than that of her mate. When the mate leaves, she is devastated. This is not just one of a sense of loss or broken heart, but because of a deep level of self ceases to exist. This is well illustrated in Chekov's classic tale of Olenka in his short story "The Darling." Dr. Deutsch is reported to have said if she had read Chekov's story first, she would not have needed to write her treatise on the borderline personality.

Melanie Kline described the object splitting of the borderline. "Object" in this case refers to the object of one's love or affection whether it is a mother, lover, child or therapist. The borderline will "split" an object into the good parts and the bad parts. The object takes on the characteristics of being all good or all evil. In the metaphor, the infant will accept and love the mother with "good breast" and reject that very same mother with the "bad breast."

The inner self is so underdeveloped that the loss in a relationship is compounded to the point of unacceptability even to the point of suicide. Psychoanalytic theory continues that there might not even be an actual loss in relationship but perhaps just a perceived or feared loss. This can be exemplified by the movie "Fatal Attraction" where the female character becomes a virtual homicidal maniac in response to the rejection by a man with whom she had a casual affair. "I will not be ignored" is the understated theme of this character. Anyone who has any kind of experience with borderline patients understands that they will not be ignored.

The term "splitting" has become confused with another behavior seen by manipulative patients on psychiatric wards. Whereas the classical splitting alternately involves glorifying and then vilifying the same individual, splitting on the psychiatric ward is generally meant to imply the purposeful creation of an antagonism among ward staff. An example of this would be a patient telling one of the nurses that another staff member said the patient could go out on the patio and smoke and not go to therapy group when, in actuality, the other staff member said no such thing. The desired effect is to get the nursing staff battling with each other, the result of which is some degree of amusement for the patient. This is not really splitting in the classical borderline sense, although it is an obnoxious habit. In one sense this is a borderline behavior because borderlines love to stir up the pot. Commotion seems to validate their existence.

On the other hand, it is not unusual for bipolar spectrum patients to be agitated and irritable and with some degree of suicidal tendencies. They may not have responded well to antidepressant medication. Sometimes when patients are irritable and perhaps tearful and talking about suicide, despite the treatment team's best efforts, it can be seen as an affront of the treatment team and, therefore, such patients must have borderline personalities.

Diane: Just Another "Suicidal Borderline"?

When I first met Diane she was sitting quietly in the day room dressed in a clean sweater and blue jeans. In her left hand she was holding a paperback novel and was twirling her long brown hair with her right hand. She was wearing nicely applied makeup, which is generally not the habit of women on an inpatient psychiatric unit. Basically, she did not appear to be a psychiatric patient. She was anxious and tense but not at all out of control. She greeted me pleasantly. Despite the fact that she made an impulsive suicide attempt the night before, she was reasonably courteous and calm under the circumstances. She appeared quite normal except for the fact that she had a gauze dressing about her left wrist and a few visible scratches on the under surface of her right wrist not covered with bandages.

As is often the curious case, a patient on the psychiatry ward in the morning appears as a tranquil sea compared to the tempest tossed storm of the previous night. It is not unusual to read the chaotic preliminary history, then see that same person not presenting with any particular psychiatric symptoms, at least not the type that would warrant keeping someone in the hospital against her will. I was warned by the nursing staff that, although she was looking "superficially bright," she was not ready to go because she was "not working on her issues."

I had always been taught that borderline patients need only brief hospitalizations and should be discharged as soon as possible lest they become somehow entrenched in the hospital as if it were a womb. Diane told me she was really ready to go and needed to get back to work which was the main stabilizing influence in her life. I did not see much point in keeping a woman in the hospital who was not presenting with any current symptoms, even though she had plenty the night before, so we cut a deal. I told her I was going to let her go home, but she had to allow me a full diagnostic interview so that perhaps we could get some type of handle on her problems which had not been previously considered. As it turned out she was all too happy to talk about herself, but it took a fair amount of patience on my part to structure the interview so as to obtain the information for which I was looking. Certainly there was the history of the drug abuse, which at first she minimized but then became more open and honest about as I persisted with my questions. There was some history of financial problems. There were periods of irritability, euphoria, impulsiveness and periods of deep depression in which would become suicidal but never make any actual serious attempts. Complicating the analysis with what was going on with Diane was the fact that she had intermittently abused amphetamines and cocaine. It is difficult to distinguish actual symptoms of psychiatric illness from withdrawal symptoms from drugs. After a period of using amphetamines it is not uncommon to "crash" or to become very sleepy, lose energy and become quite depressed. As addicts know, to combat this crashing phenomenon, they will take more drugs. But sooner or later the piper has to be paid and the period of agitated exhaustion ensues. There certainly was some of this in Diane's history. There was also a history of alcohol abuse which was clear from her history and the history of her formerly treating psychiatrist. With an individual such as Diane, it is important to figure out not just that she abuses drugs, but why and what was the effect she was looking for. Was she using drugs and alcohol to treat some underlying symptoms? Or was it just a means to an end? Or was it a social issue? Was it a pure addiction? That is, did she start using a substance, enjoy it, continue to use it and enjoy it, and then get "hooked?" Other questions to ask would include finding out at what age she started abusing drugs and why. Also, it would be important to know if there were periods of sobriety and what her mood states were like during these periods and what led to the relapse. None of this information was on her psychological record and without it, many physicians and therapists would find it easy to dismiss Diane as a "drug abusing borderline." Perhaps this is the case, but since she is a young woman with the likelihood of living another half century, she deserves every consideration that we as mental health professionals can give her before she passes on from therapist to therapist and doctor to doctor as the burn out in sequence. Beyond all the psychiatric and medical history taking are the issues (perhaps the ones she is "not working on") about childhood, upbringing and trauma which may have affected her behavior and moods over the years.

As is often the case, there was copious historical information about the circumstances of her upbringing including the divorce of her parents when she was six years old and some verbal abuse by a stepfather whom her mother married when Diane was eight. There was also some sexual abuse by a stepbrother who was six years older than she. This involved a few episodes of fondling but no sexual penetration. It would be unfair to Diane to say that she had not "worked on her issues" since she had been in therapy for four or five years and had repeatedly gone over these issues with her therapist. It did not appear that dredging up these issues once again would further promote her journey into health.

During the diagnostic interview process, Diane did sometimes become tearful but, within minutes, could become fairly calm or even bright. This "lability of affect" is sometimes seen as quite characteristic of borderline patients.

It would be good to know what her moods are like, how she experiences them and what sets them off. And what about the promiscuity? Is this a moral issue, a character issue, something that drives her? What is her sexual experience? Does she seek sex or just use sex as a way to be cared for by men?

She has a history of non-compliance with medication. What has made her noncompliant? What is her attitude about medication? Despite years of treatment and interface with the mental health system and county crisis system, none of this information had ever been obtained.

Diane was eager to get help and answer questions that had never been asked of her before. It was most important to distinguish whether or not Diane had a bipolar disorder, or exhibited a borderline personality disorder. The treatment implications would be quite different. Sometimes people can actually have both disorders, but even so, treatment can be vastly improved if we know exactly with what we are dealing.

Diane's pre vious treating physicians and therapists avoided bipolar diagnosis with her based on a number of factors:

1)   She never had a manic episode.
2)   She was sexually molested in childhood.
3)   She came from a broken home.
4)   She is very co-dependent.
5)   She is an alcohol and substance abuser.
6)   No one ever asked the right questions.
7)   No one thought about it.

As Dr. Jay Amsterdam of the Department of Psychiatry of the University of Pennsylvania once put it, to not diagnose bipolar disorder because someone never had a manic episode is like not diagnosing diabetes because the patient was never hospitalized with acute diabetic ketoacidosis.

A trial of Depakote here would also be possibly diagnostic. If Diane tried this and found over the long haul that her moods were starting to stabilize, we might be able to diagnose based on response to treatment. That may seem to be a bit backwards, but in psychiatry as in other branches of medicine, sometimes diagnosis is made by the process of exclusion. However, we are not strictly dealing with exclusion here. We are also dealing with significant observable features of a psychiatric syndrome which is, according to the American Psychiatric Association, characteristically underdiagnosed or misdiagnosed.

Sometimes it takes "elixir of time and essence of patience" to really figure out whether or not this is going to be a useful treatment. Although Diane may calm down within a few days, the real proof of the effectiveness will not be evident for perhaps three to six months. It takes a willing and conscientious physician to ride the next several months with her down this rocky road. More likely than not there will be relapses in drug and alcohol abuse, but they will get less likely as time goes on. As they say at Alcoholics Anonymous, "Relapse is part of recovery."

Suppose it turns out Diane really does not have a bipolar disorder? She still may very well respond to a mood stabilizer such as Depakote or lithium either alone or in combination with a small dose of antidepressant medication. In considering the risk to benefit ratio of trying a medication, certainly the benefits outweigh the risks here. There is certainly a risk that she will not respond to this treatment, but that cannot be determined for several months.

I have met many patients like Diane who have had bipolar disorder considered in the past who say that, as far as Depakote and lithium are concerned, they have "been there, done that." But careful analysis of the history may further reveal the trial was short lived and inadequate. A one month trial may be of relatively little use especially if the medication was combined with high doses of antidepressants.

Individuals with borderline personality disorder may have numerous traits which overlap with the spectrum of bipolar disorders. The relationship among various psychiatric disorders is quite complex. Various diagnostic entities do not stand neatly alone but often involve a great deal of what is known as comorbidity. Depression and insecurity go hand in hand.

Dependent Personality Disorder, which is a diagnosable entity from the diagnostic and statistical manual, has a strong correlation with depression. If an individual has the symptoms of mood instability in the context of the borderline personality disorder, should not the person be treated? Should not that treatment also involve medication for which the need may be essential and possibly even permanent. Complicating the medical treatment of the borderline patient is the fact that such patients often resist medication, take it incompletely, or even, when most compliant with medications, sometimes do not respond well to treatment. The impulsiveness of the borderline patient may make the medication which is supposed to be a factor in healing into an actual liability. It is the nightmare of every prescribing psychiatrist to see a patient overdose on a prescribed medication. Sometimes we get into a double bind whereby providing the necessary medication provides a significant risk, but denying the medication also leads to risks. Even today there is a certain degree of political incorrectness to taking psychiatric medications. This may cause both the patient and the clinician to resist the use of proper treatment.

We know that proper treatment of bipolar persons leads to substantial decreases in alcoholism, substance abuse, divorce and unemployment. A lot of what appears to be related to unstable character often has underlying medical psychiatric issues which, in Diane's case, turned out to be a bipolar disorder. Depakote turned out to be very helpful in allowing her to remain focused and productive. Unfortunately, she gained about twenty pounds, but has lost about half this since she recently switched to a newer mood stabilizer, lamotrigine. She continues to do well at her job and is in a stable relationship.

Now we do not have to dismiss this woman as a "dysfunctional border-line." Still, even with our sophisticated diagnostic techniques, we have limitations in attempting to describe an individual who really has a con-stellation of behaviors, thoughts and perceptions that are uniquely hers.

Chapter Eight

Kindling

Until recently, common wisdom in the mental health professions held that there were two main types of depression; that which is caused by situational factors known as "exogenous depression" and that which is caused by internal biological factors, "endogenous depression." The basic assumption was that horrible, traumatic incidents in earlier life would predispose an individual to develop depression in later life. Examples would include: having been molested as a child, issues around parental divorce, serious accident or injury, or the loss of a loved one. More recent or immediate events which may have triggered a depressive or agitated episode are known as precipitating events. A decent psychiatric and social history will explore how these recent and remote factors affect somebody's current mood state.

The problem with this dichotomy is that it represents an attempt to make a clear separation between depression arising from situational factors from those due to internal biologic factors.

That would lead a lot of practitioners to believe if someone walks into their office with misfortunes approaching that of the biblical Job, and that patient has rather severe depression which appears to be caused by all of his problems, then the need to search for other factors causing the depression is no longer necessary. But the truth is, the interaction between stress and trauma and the mood state of any given individual is rather complex.

Throughout much of the history of psychiatry and psychotherapy, it had been common wisdom that the treatment of nervous and mental disorders should focus on understanding early childhood trauma, and perhaps more recent stresses. Healing would be derived from discussing and learning about and understanding early trauma in life so the patient could grow, mature, and move beyond depression and anxiety. This is called the dynamic approach.

Over the last two decades, there has been a significant trend for psychiatry to move into the biologic realm; that is, the new understanding of depression and altered mood states is really a biologic issue. Understanding the chemistry of the nervous system and how to correct congenital imbalances would really prove to be the key to long term mental health. There developed a split and somewhat of an antagonism between the dynamic and biologic camps. The therapists would look upon the physicians as mere "pill pushers" who sometimes had to be tolerated, since some people really did seem to need to be on medication. Psychiatrists, who are physicians, would find themselves in the back rooms of mental health centers and private clinics writing prescriptions while the real business of getting it on with mental health would be found in the individual and group therapy rooms. A certain degree of disdain and scorn would be directed toward the medically oriented psychiatrists which was further amplified by a certain degree of resentment since the physicians were still getting paid considerably higher than non-medical therapists.

Psychiatrists, on the other hand, would often express scorn for non-medical therapists who seemed to gain ego and financial gratification from keeping one foot stuck in the nineteenth century. Psychiatrists would find themselves being pushed aside and out of the therapist's position by legions of trained therapists who were not in the medical profession.

The sense of conflict and territoriality was exemplified in a colleague's statement several years ago when he was discussing the difference between the biologic psychiatrist as "one who basically diagnoses and prescribes" and psychotherapists. "A biological psychiatrist will have his patients doing better in two or three weeks while a therapist will still have his patients shelling out for treatment two or three years down the road."

Supposedly intelligent psychologists who are lobbying to be able to write prescriptions, even though they are not medically trained, argue that antidepressants or mood stabilizing medications are okay while the patient is in the early stages of therapy, so he can have his mood stabilized. They further argue that, once the mood is stabilized through the magic of psychotherapy, he will not need the medication anymore. This is only partially true and ignores significant biologic and medical factors.

As research continues, we are finding out that both camps have merits and flaws in their arguments. What we are learning through recent research is that trauma in early life can indeed predispose somebody to have psychiatric difficulties in later life. But also, not everybody is the same, and some of us have more of a biologic trigger than others. It is certainly well documented that genetics and family history play a significant role in the development of various bipolar disorders. There is no clear cut line between nature and nurture since dysfunctional and agitated bipolar parents have an increased risk of having their own children developing depression or dysfunctional behavior later in life.

So the question is, does a child growing up in a home with fighting, arguing, physical abuse, and alcoholism have a more likely chance of having that as his own lifestyle when he is an adult, based on genetic factors or from the fact that he was repeatedly traumatized psychologically as a child and thereby will more likely have significant problems himself.?

And what about treatment? Psychotherapy treatment outcome studies have indicated that there are numerous disorders that respond just as well to psychotherapy as respond to medications. However, the response to medication plus therapy combined exceeds that of either type of treatment given alone. There are many depressive patients who would just as soon "go to the doctor, get my prescription and leave." Such an attitude may reflect the preference of the patient seeking treatment for depression to be seen as having a medical condition as opposed to a psychiatric condition and needing a "shrink." Also HMOs and other health plans would like to encourage this type of thinking since three or four prescription appointments per year are a lot cheaper than twenty or forty therapy appointments. Yet, it is most important that we as a society understand that depression and bipolar disorders are very serious conditions which take an enormous toll in the cost to individual human beings and to society in general. Cutting a few dollars here and there today will only cost us infinitely more tomorrow.

The concept of kindling derives from the metaphor of using small pieces of dried wood to start a larger fire burning. The kindling wood may long be consumed but the larger campfire may burn through the night, and perhaps lead to an uncontrolled forest fire. So it is with precipitating and predisposing factors leading to depression, particularly in the context of bipolar disorders. As has been pointed out, the majority of bipolar episodes are precipitated by some type of traumatic event. From the psychotherapist's point of view, the patient becoming more stable depends on "working on the issues" involved in the precipitating event or trauma. What often happens, though, is the precipitating event, whether it is a divorce, losing one's job, death in the family, or perhaps the fourteenth break up with a girlfriend, could be the match that lights the dry twig in a tinder box ready to burn.

Experimental studies with rats have shown that stresses such as electric shocks introduced early in life lead to increased periods of agitation and irritability later in life. The more traumatized the rat is before maturity, the less stimulation it takes to agitate the rat once it reaches maturity. In a sense, the nervous system can be trained to respond vigorously to trauma and, the more trauma there is early on, the less trauma it takes to invoke a response later on. There is emerging evidence that this is true for human beings as well. In bipolar patients, each successive bipolar episode is less likely to be brought on by psychological trauma. Eventually, episodes requiring treatment may not have been brought on by any observable trauma at all. As a matter of fact, each serious episode of agitated depression, or psychosis, is an actual physical trauma which predisposes the patient to having an even more significant problem the next time which, in all probability, will occur sooner. The more serious the breakdowns, the more likely he or she will have even further breakdowns. That is why staying on medications and continuing treatment are of the utmost importance to anybody being treated for a bipolar disorder.

Another poorly understood element in the treatment of severe bipolar episodes is the resistance of the nervous system to respond to medication which was quite useful until it was stopped. If, for example, lithium or Depakote has been very useful in keeping a patient stable, and a person, for whatever reason, decides to stop the medication, and then over time deteriorates into a state requiring time off work or even hospitalization, there is a very good possibility that particular medication will not work again. It is as if the nervous system had reached a harmony with the lithium or Depakote or, in some cases, medications like Prozac or Paxil, but the harmony is destroyed with the withdrawal of the medication. The person relapses into a serious depressive or agitated state or perhaps even into psychosis more serious than before, and the medications which could always be counted on in the past become of little or no value now. Each serious episode just seems to make the kindling wood drier and more ready to explode in flame at the slightest spark. The challenge for the bipolar patient is to see that the spark does not get a chance to reignite. Even the best and most conscientious efforts, however, do not always prevent a relapse. But sometimes an alert, educated patient knows when things are starting to go downhill, even though he is complying completely with the medication. That is the time to share this information with his doctor.

There are many individuals who have had one serious manic episode and become stabilized on medication and lead normal lives. Until recently, it would not be unusual for a patient in consultation with his physician to try to taper off the mood stabilizing medication. After all, if someone has not had a problem for five or ten years, why stay on medication for the rest of his life. The question is now being answered, because most patients run a high likelihood of relapsing into serious psychiatric conditions within a year after discontinuing medications. And not only that, but the relapse will be worse than the previous illness and the medications that had been working for years may not be of any effect at all.

Darlene; Bravery In the Face of Tragedy

Darlene is a thirty-nine year old woman who presented with a very dramatic case history. Three years ago her family was involved in a deadly motor vehicle accident. Her husband and her two sons, ages ten and twelve, were killed instantly. Her surviving daughter, now age eleven, requires wheelchair assistance for the rest of her life. The drunk driver of the other vehicle had liability insurance for $30,000 which was all she eventually received. He spent two years in jail and has since been released. Her daughter receives income from Social Security since her father is deceased and because of her disabilities. Still, Darlene has to work full time to make ends meet. Although her daughter, Kimberly, attends public schools, Darlene is quite overwhelmed with the logistics of getting her home from school, getting help from some relatives, and hiring a companion to help out with Kimberly while Darlene still has to be at work.

For most of the time since the accident, Darlene has had serious depression. She has made three suicide attempts in the last three years, but comes into the hospital now because of one more attempt whereby she took an overdose of medication and also cut her wrists. She has been on three or four different kinds of medication, all of which helped a little, but only temporarily at best. If ever there was a clear reason for someone to have serious depression, surely this is it.

When I met Darlene in the hospital the morning after her admission, she appeared as a braver and more gracious woman than I could have imagined. I expected her to express her profound grief, how it had burdened her and destroyed her life. But that is not what I heard. She acknowledged that, yes, her life had been torn apart by the loss of most of her family. And yet, she had her injured daughter who was completely mentally capable and actually functioning well in school. There was her dog and cat, who certainly gave her some pleasure. And after three years she was also starting to develop a relationship with a man who had been very good to her and Kimberly. As much as had been taken from her, she also acknowledged there were some things to live for. Then why the suicide attempts? She explained "sometimes I do just fine; I know I'll always have sadness in my heart for my family that is gone, but I'm able to do what I can do. But many times I don't sleep, and I can't focus and I just want to jump out of my skin. That's the part I can't stand."

So I had to ask myself, was this case really a no brainer? That is, were the historical facts so clear and obvious that there was not really that much to figure out? Could simple pills help heal this woman's broken life? So far, there had not been much success with this element of treatment. Ongoing, routine counseling and therapy also seemed to provide some level of comfort for her. So what else could be done?

Twenty-two years ago, Darlene had been hospitalized for about five days for a suicide attempt by overdose. It was not a serious attempt, as she had only taken a handful of some nontoxic pills. However, she recalls she was very depressed over the breakup with a boyfriend to whom she thought she would be engaged. At around age thirty she had another hospitalization after having some significant stresses in the workplace. Her children were very young at the time and her mother-in-law had moved in to help as she was not very capable of taking care of her children for several months. At that time she had a lot of insomnia and difficulty focusing.

Darlene further recalled that throughout the years she has had periods of high energy whereby she was able to get a lot of work done during the nights and evenings when everyone else was asleep. She enjoyed having all this energy since she had three children and was able to get cooking, laundry and cleaning done in the middle of the night and felt this was her own very private time. There were periods of depression when she would stay in bed for much of the weekend and her husband would have to take care of the kids while she was resting and recuperating.

Further history revealed that Darlene's father was alcoholic and very abusive, although she was never sexually molested. Her father's brother had committed suicide but she does not really remember very many details about this. One thing she never revealed before is that, over the past several years, she had been smoking marijuana from time to time because it helped her calm down and get some rest. She denied any use of amphetamines or cocaine. She had a drink only on occasion.

Immediately after the accident when she lost her husband and two sons, she was stunned, but ultimately able to make funeral arrangements and deal with attorneys, etc. She was working part tie and took a three month leave of absence with the support of her employer. She was actually able to return to work, although she was quite depressed and shortly thereafter started on antidepressant medication. Her heart was heavy but she was able to carry on. Sometimes at work she would burst into tears when she least expected to, but after a quick trip to the ladies room she was able to compose herself and return to work. The irritability started to creep in about six months after the accident. Her sleep had been reasonable although not great. There were a lot of times when she would wake up at night but, after a little while, would be able to go back to sleep. Now she was not getting any sleep at all and spent a lot of nights up pacing, wringing her hands and crying. Not long after that she got some marijuana from some friends and this did help her get back to sleep some, but she was not feeling very rested. She was able to make out a schedule with some help from friends and family. A private nursing company was able to care for Kimberly during her absences so she could continue on with her job.

Sometimes the irritability and agitation seemed to come on very suddenly and the grief with which she was dealing would come back with great intensity. She would feel totally overwhelmed and distraught and at these times she would be very impulsive. On one occasion she cut herself and on another she overdosed on pills. Both times she went to the hospital and both times she was feeling remorseful about her behavior and was sent home, with the proviso that she attend outpatient counseling which she did.

I called her outpatient therapist and discussed the possibility that maybe the medications were making things worse instead of better and perhaps different medications may be more useful. I brought up the possibility there may have been a mild mood cycling disorder that was present prior to the death of her family and that the trauma kindled a mood cycling event which has been continuing because of the activating affect of the antidepressant. Her therapist was very open to the idea and generally did not like the concept of her patients being on medication in the first place. I told her I thought it would be a risk, but perhaps we could take her off the antidepressant medication and see what happens, particularly since she was in the hospital, although I did not plan to keep her there for very long. Darlene agreed with this strategy and revealed to me that several years ago, before the accident, a therapist suggested to her that she might be manic depressive.

Without the antidepressants, Darlene calmed down fairly quickly and was able to sleep better. Eventually, she did well with just a little bit if antidepressant in combination with lithium. Naturally, she continued with sadness in her life but was able to cope and care for her daughter.

Darlene continued in treatment with her outpatient therapist and psychiatrist. I had not heard from her for about two years until recently I received a postcard. She shared with me that she was engaged and was going to marry the whom she had been seeing. Her daughter was mainstreamed at the regular high school, was doing well and hoping to go to college. Fortunately, her treating psychiatrist followed her very closely and was very clear with her that she needed to continue with her medications, particularly lithium.

Darlene's case is an example of a situation where the circumstances and events seem so obvious that much digging or exploration is not necessary. But tragic circumstances can happen to anyone. Just because someone has an underlying mood cycling disorder does not render her immune to personal catastrophe. If Darlene's bipolar spectrum disorder had not been recognized, perhaps the tragedy that befell her family would have been compounded. This was a rather extreme case of situational events "kindling" her depression and agitation. Certainly, less dramatic events can also kindle mood cycling and instability. In Darlene's case, it was not just the medication that helped her recover, but the combination of medication and supportive counseling and therapy. She also sought comfort and support from an intimate relationship in her personal life. These factors combined helped sustain her through the storm.

Sometimes there are factors beyond what we consider psychiatric, such as grace, courage and faith. In keeping her life balanced, Darlene will be able to survive, even though in the past she was not so sure. It is the combination of these factors which help to dampen the kindling and allow healing to continue.

Chapter Nine

Too Much of a Good Thing

Harriet is a thirty-five year old woman who has had problems with depression and mood cycling since her early twenties. She has a history of alcohol abuse but has been clean and sober for the last four years since she started treatment with a combination of lithium and antidepressants. Her main problem over the years was deep depression which would come and go and was often accompanied by agitation and irritability. She did not tolerate Depakote very well because of extreme weight gain, but fortunately she seemed to do well with lithium. Overall she was fairly stable and able to go to work and miss very little time because of depression.

About a year ago she sank into a fairly deep depression and her physician started her on Zoloft. Zoloft is a very good antidepressant which seemed to be well tolerated with few side effects. Harriet started to improve and was feeling quite well after bout three weeks on the Zoloft. She continued on this medication and physician told her he thought it was best if she continued taking it. About six months ago she began to deteriorate into a deeper depression and the Zoloft was increased to 100 milligrams which, in general, is a mid-range dose for most depressed patients. Her response was less than optimal and the dose was further increased to 150 mg. Her sleep pattern began to deteriorate and there were many nights where she felt she could not sleep at all or perhaps get just a few hours. A mild sleeping pill was prescribed which seemed to help a little, but after a few weeks she found she needed to take more and more of these sleeping pills beyond what was recommended. Finally she started drinking once again. She felt very guilty about this since it had been almost four years since she had any alcohol. She would drink a half bottle of wine before going to sleep. She insisted the wine was only to help her sleep and not because she enjoyed drinking. Soon, however, she was drinking a full bottle of wine every evening. As is often the case with alcohol, she was able to get to sleep but would wake up in the middle of the night feeling more agitated and shaky than ever.

She was getting into more arguments at work and was "written up" by her supervisor on three occasions in the previous two months. Her attendance at work became more sporadic and she was in danger of losing her job. She was referred by her family physician to a psychiatrist who felt the diagnosis of bipolar disorder was probably wrong and that she, in fact, had an agitated depression. Nonetheless, she remained on the lithium and Zoloft. The antipsychotic drug Haldol was added since this is often used for patients who are not psychotic but highly moody and turbulent who need to be sedated. She was able to get a few hours sleep once Haldol 5 mg was added to her medication regimen. When the Haldol was increased to 10 mg she was able to get more sleep, but then was unable to get up in the morning and found herself very groggy. Harriet became quite restless and would often be up at night pacing around her apartment. She was contemplating suicide and had made a vague plan by saving up some pills and fantasized about taking a large amount of them along with a bottle of wine. Apparently the Zoloft was not working very well anymore, but her psychiatrist had been aware of a technique where adding a second antidepressant could boost the effect of the first antidepressant and had seen this work well before. So now Harriet was on two antidepressants and an antipsychotic agent but was doing worse than ever.

One evening, her husband reported she was becoming argumentative, combative and was possibly hallucinating and talking about suicide. She began breaking dishes in the kitchen one evening with no apparent precipitating event. After she became aggressive, her husband called the police who had to restrain her and she was transported to her local emergency room where she was placed on a commitment and referred to a psychiatric hospital unit. The emergency room doctor consulted with her psychiatrist who seemed rather bewildered by the situation saying she had been doing well but deteriorated. He felt the problem was that she was developing a major depression with psychotic features, which is an official diagnosis from the DSM IV. He also offered to consult with the attending psychiatrist at the inpatient psychiatric ward to give some history about Harriet's case. The treating psychiatrist wanted to make it clear he did not think she had a bipolar disorder since she never really was manic in the past and that she had been on lithium and Depakote which had not seemed effective.

When Harriet reached the hospital, she was assigned to an astute, young psychiatric resident whose training focused on psychopharmacology. The resident suspected Harriet was bipolar after all and that the problem was not that the lithium did not work, but that the antidepressants destabilized her, causing her to become more irritable and manic. Lithium is not the favored drug to treat bipolar spectrum disorders and the increases in antidepressants allowed the irritability and hypomanic symptoms to "break through" the lithium and cause her to develop increasing bipolar symptoms. The matter was made worse when the lithium was stopped and compounded even further by the addition of an antipsychotic drug and another antidepressant. Although the Haldol did allow her to get some sleep, it also caused some restlessness which is a quite common side effect with this type of drug. This is what led to the increased pacing. This is a case where everything was going wrong and all the attempts to fix the problem actually made them worse. The resident's first maneuver was to make sure all the antidepressants were stopped.

Since Harriet was in the hospital being observed, it was safe to do this. He felt since she was hallucinating and very agitated, a little bit of antipsychotic drug could remain on board and some sleeping medication added so she could start to recover as her sleep-wake cycle would return to normal. He played a hunch, but there was very little to lose here and, as it turned out, the hunch was correct. Within twenty-four hours Harriet was much calmer although somewhat groggy. Within forty-eight hours the hallucinations were entirely gone and she was sleeping through the night with the assistance of a mild sleeping pill. At times, she was a little disoriented from the assault on her sense and sensibilities from the last several months. On the third day she was started on one of the newer mood stabilizers, lamotrigene, which is also known under the trade name Lamictal. Although she had been out of work for six weeks, she received some assistance from the social work department in regaining her job, utilizing information about the Family Leave Act and the American's with Disabilities Act. Upon leaving the hospital on day five, Harriet was referred to the hospital's outpatient program. She was educated on the use of antidepressants. Even though she responded very poorly to the antidepressants, it was certainly conceivable that in the future she may need them should she cycle down into a deep depression. It should be pointed out that it is certainly a case, once again, of "less is more" when it comes to antidepressants. A small, temporary dose is much more useful than large, combined doses of antidepressants, particularly with Harriet's type of mood cycling disorder.

There is one other sticky part of the epilogue to this story. Although things worked out for Harriet, the resident had difficulty relaying his treatment strategy to the referring psychiatrist. Although not an academic psychiatrist, the referring psychiatrist did have a courtesy faculty position and it is always somewhat difficult for a resident to be advising a more senior colleague on the best way to treat a patient. The resident did approach the telephone call with a certain degree of deference. The referring psychiatrist politely listened and thanked him and suggested that perhaps any change in medications can improve a patient. He added that certainly we cannot underestimate the therapeutic value of the "structure" of the inpatient psychiatric unit. By the end of the conversation the junior doctor felt assured that his senior colleague would be providing his psychiatric unit with plenty of business in the future.

Chapter Ten

Postpartum Depression
The Case of Alice

Alice, a twenty-six year old woman, was hospitalized on an involuntary hold after she overdosed on thirty tablets of amitriptyline (also known as Elavil).

Alice was a single mother who had given birth three months ago. The father of the child was an angry, abusing, irresponsible man. Three months before the birth, he said he really did not want anything to do with her or the baby and left the state. She realized in the long run it was the best thing for the father of her child to be out of her life and out of her child's life. Her parents were angry and somewhat punitive toward Alice, but as the time of birth approached, they realized this would be their grandchild and became more supportive and allowed Alice to live at home with them. Two months after the birth of the child, Alice seemed to sink into a significant depression. Her sleep became poor, she was lethargic and she began overeating. She was referred to her HMO psychiatrist by her obstetrician who ultimately diagnosed her as having an "adjustment disorder with depressed mood." Upon starting Elavil, she became considerably brighter within the first few days. The lethargy seemed to completely disappear. She was taking good care of her child and did not seem tired at all. As a matter of fact, within the next week or so she began to need much less sleep and was up in the middle of the night doing chores, writing plans, cleaning the house, cooking and generally keeping quite busy. During the day she would entertain friends on the telephone about her baby, even seeking out and calling friends she had not spoken with for years. She was quite pleased with her psychiatrist and his brilliance in prescribing her medication.

About a month later, Alice began to experience depression once again. But the depression would not last all day. She might feel depressed in the morning and even be tearful and ruminative and by afternoon would be bright and cheerful once again, but the moods would become erratic. She would take to her bed sometimes in the late afternoon, only to be bounding out of bed at 9:00 or 10:00 p.m. to do more chores. Sometimes suggestions from her mother would be met with agitated outbursts. On two separate occasions Alice broke dishes purposefully on the most minor provocations. At the urging of her parents, she returned to see the psychiatrist who agreed the problem was beginning to worsen and the stresses and strains of single motherhood were getting to her. He advised her to increase the antidepressant medication slightly and also added a mild tranquilizer. For a few nights Alice did get a little more sleep but then started staying up late again. Her mothering skills became even worse and Grandma had to pitch in even more than before. This was more than Alice's mother had bargained for and was becoming quite resentful having to take over mothering duties at her age.

On the night before her admission to the hospital Alice and her mother got into a loud verbal tiff. Alice was responding to her mother's criticisms with a rather significant temper tantrum. It ended with Alice kicking over a chair and loudly retreating to her room with a slam of the door. Things remained fairly quiet in Alice's room and at that point her mother became alarmed when Alice did not answer her door when she knocked. When she entered the room, Alice was on her bed snoring very loudly with an empty pill bottle at her side. Alice's mother called 911 and Alice was transported to the nearest emergency room. Her stomach was pumped and, fortunately, most of the pills were retrieved. After observation overnight, she was quite alert and somewhat remorseful about her behavior but, nonetheless, she was placed on a legal hold and sent to the psychiatry department. Her admitting diagnosis was "postpartum depression." At first glance this seemed to be a reasonably easy and logical deduction. She was three months postpartum and this was her first ever suicide attempt.

However, after some careful history taking was initiated, it was clear there were some other factors which had not been previously considered. For example, Alice had had some intermittent depressions prior to having her child or becoming pregnant. These were depressions of a significant nature, not just a day or two of the blues or premenstrual syndrome. Ever since her early teen years she had periods of significant depression which would last several days and perhaps lead to her staying home from school and take to her bed sometimes feigning illness of a physical nature. These depressions would come and go. Her mother was very helpful at giving some history and recalls that, during her junior year in high school, Alice was one of the most popular and active girls in her class. She had made the cheerleading squad that year and was active in the college prep club. Alice recalls that was the best year of her life in terms of mood. Her grades were better than ever, and she was making plans to go on to college after graduation.

During her senior year her grades slipped somewhat, although she still was a relatively good student. However, she became more absorbed in extracurricular activities and even became somewhat sexually promiscuous. During that year she became pregnant and had an abortion which led to intermittent feelings of guilt. Her recent outpatient psychiatrist felt this significantly contributed to her depression.

As it turned out, Alice indeed had a postpartum depression, but what no one realized up until this point was that a very large percentage of postpartum depressions are a signal event in a life history of bipolar disorder. At least thirty percent of postpartum depressions are really a bipolar event. Some authorities believe the actual percentage is considerably higher. One of the research criteria used at the National Institute of Mental Health in identifying bipolar disorder is postpartum depression. Also, actual psychotic experiences which involved true manic episodes in the postpartum period are usually manic episodes. It was clear from the history that Alice suffered with a long-term bipolar disorder which became more evident during the postpartum period.

In the hospital, the antidepressant medication was withheld and Alice was started on Depakote. Within the first two days she again was able to calm down quite considerably. She was still feeling a significant amount of depression, however, so she was started on a low dose of an alternative antidepressant. The plan was for her to be watched very carefully to make sure no signs or symptoms of agitation or irritability redeveloped. She was discharged after five days, fairly calm, able to sleep well and, although she remained somewhat depressed, there was no evidence of any suicidal thoughts or plans. She felt comforted to be able to care for her young child. However, she was advised not to continue breastfeeding because the medication can pass into breast milk. Also, she agreed to follow up with a support group for single mothers which she found very helpful. Alice remains in treatment and is doing well with her child and husband.

While postpartum depression can be a bipolar event, postpartum psychosis which involves bizarre thinking and behavior, is usually a manic episode. Simple investigation can usually clarify the situation and lead to a good treatment outcome.

Chapter Eleven

Bipolar, Sell High

Bipolar and Regular (Unipolar) Depression

Similarities

Unipolar Depression	*Bipolar Depression*
1. Depression may recur	1. Depression may recur
2. Sleep disturbance	2. Sleep disturbance
3. Appetite disturbance	3. Appetite disturbance
4. Suicide risk	4. Suicide risk
5. Thought disorder when severe	5. Thought disorder when severe
6. May be family history of depression	6. May be family history of depression
7. Can be associated with substance abuse	7. Can be associated with substance abuse
8. Impairs ability to function	8. Impairs ability to function
9. Responds to proper treatment	9. Responds to proper treatment

Bipolar and Regular (Unipolar) Depression

Differences

Unipolar

1. Average onset late 30s to early 40s
2. Not associated with cycling

3. Worrying, ruminative thoughts
4. Low energy
5. Isolation or withdrawal
6. Responds well to antidepressants
7. Not associated with aggression or violence

Bipolar

1. Average onset late teens to early 20s
2. Associated with agitation and irritability
3. Racing thoughts
4. Energy low or increased
5. Engages in risky or intrusive behaviors
6. Uneven response to antidepressants
7. Can be associated with explosive and irritable behavior

Bipolar disorder is not a term that describes or defines a single entity. The term bipolar spectrum was delineated by Hagob Akiskal, M.D. in his seminal 1983 paper describing the various disorders. For someone to say they have a bipolar disorder can only give a very general indication of the type of problem since there is a whole spectrum of severity from mild to extraordinarily psychotic. The term spectrum is utilized since the term implies multiple colors and shadings along a continuum. Also, the bipolar disorders often do not occur alone, but in conjunction with numerous other psychiatric conditions. It is extremely important to recognize whether or not a depression is really part of a bipolar disorder. This understanding is essential in leading to the proper treatment since unrecognized bipolar depression, when treated as a regular depression, will often lead to treatment relapse failure or perhaps eve worsening of the condition. The most important part in saving people's lives, or at least the productivity of their lives, is the understanding that the casual diagnosis of depression is often incorrect and leads to frequent tragic consequences. Such consequences may not be an overt suicide but a life of poor functioning, low productivity, and chaotic and unstable relationships.

Generally, it is the depression that brings the patient to the doctor's office and not the hyperactivity. Although such hyperactivity may feel irritable and unpleasant to patients, they often feel that such subjective experience is normal. Although not always the case, during periods of excessive energy or hyperactivity, there may be a feeling of well being, euphoria, perhaps a natural high or "buzz" with extra energy and this feels quite positive. Most people will not seek treatment for feeling too well. When excessive activity evolves into frank mania, the patient may feel especially good, although his observed behavior by others is quite psychotic or bizarre and often requires the force of legal authorities to get him into treatment. Obviously, it is the severe depression with frequent suicidal thoughts which brings the patient in for treatment. The physician, who may have significant time constraints, may do what appears to be the easy and obvious; that is, prescribe an antidepressant or tranquilizer and hope for the best. Sometimes a cursory examination followed by a quick prescription may do just the trick, but up to half the time this just may make things worse. Below are listed numerous categories of the variations of mood cycling which are part of the bipolar spectrum. Not all of these are official diagnoses but are recognized patterns of mood which puts an individual at risk for trouble.

Note that several of the terms use the variation of the root "thymic" or "thymia" which is from the Greek referring to mood state. In ancient times it had been thought that the thymus gland located in the chest was the root of our mood states. Modern psychiatric terminology uses such terms as "dysthymia" referring to an ongoing chronic depression, "euthymia" which is basically a normal or good mood. Sometimes the word "normothymic" is used. "Hyperthymia" refers to an elevated mood which perhaps may be getting close to a hypomanic state but not quite. "Cyclothymic" obviously refers to mood cycling. "Thymoleptics" are drugs which stabilize mood.

The various levels of bipolar illness other than true manic depression were thought to be rare and even, according to the current edition of DSM, about one half to one percent of people will experience this. However, research over the last two decades, and particularly in recent years, indicates it is considerably higher and perhaps may account for half of all clinical depressions. Dr. J.A. Eggland at the American Psychiatric Association meeting in 1982 referred to the wide variety bipolar disorders as "the bipolar iceberg" to indicate that the vast majority of the bipolar disorders are subtle and submerged. Although these data have been developing since the late 1970s, the application of this information has only recently filtered its way into the front line trenches of mental health care. The following is a list of some of the variants of bipolar disorders.

Bipolar Type II

This disorder has been recognized since the late 1970s but did not become an official diagnosis until the advent of the most recent edition of the Diagnostic and Statistical Manual in 1994(the DSM IV). It remains the only official bipolar diagnosis other than true manic depressive illness which is Bipolar type I..

Bipolar type II disorder is characterized by recurrent depressions with no actual full blown mania. Instead of mania, there is buried in the history at least one episode of hypomania. A hypomanic episode is one in which there is a sustained period of increased activity. Often accompanying this episode is a significant decrease in the need for sleep. The signs of hypomania may be very subtle, and are much less intense than in a true mania. Generally, during a hypomanic episode, a person will not seek out treatment, but will probably be a source of annoyance to family and coworkers because of increased talking and distractability. This period can last for days, up to weeks. Often the person may not recall ever having had such a period unless questioned very specifically or carefully. Once started on antidepressant medication, he may become very agitated. The diagnosis is often missed because the therapist or physician does not delve deep enough or follow up properly in questioning the patient.

Dr. Akiskal and others believe that perhaps the majority of depressions seen in clinical practice, especially those that do not respond well to treatment, are really bipolar type II or one of the other bipolar depressions that have never been correctly identified. Eventually, this type of disorder may evolve into a more apparent cycling mood disorder with more frequent hypomanic episodes. As in full manic depression, depression and activation may occur together in what is known as a mixed state of agitated depression. Although mixed states are officially recognized as occurring in full blown bipolar I disorder (manic depression), there is no official acknowledgment of mixed states in the softer forms of bipolar disorders.

This is not because they don't exist, but it is because DSM-IV is behind the curve in keeping up with current research in this area.

Cyclothymic Disorder

In clyclothymia, the individual has numerous rapid mood swings. The person may have a long history of moodiness, irritability, ups and downs, periods of productivity with periods of lethargy. There are generally some periods of hypomania with excessive activity and chattiness but nothing that really looks significant. Sleep cycling may be present with periods of excessive sleeping alternating with other periods of little or no sleep without diminished energy. Individuals with this type of disorder may sometimes look as though they are hyperactive. Cyclothymic individuals will very frequently evolve into having a significant serious depression. The recognition of pre-existing cyclothymia is a very helpful clue in providing treatment once the depression cycles into a greater degree of severity. It is also possible that the cyclothymic individual may eventually develop a period of actual mania. One of the most common reasons that physicians will not diagnose a bipolar disorder is because the patient had no pre-existing mania. I have heard intelligent physicians say something such as "I don't think this person is bipolar because I really took a careful history and there was no previous history of mania." Needless to say, the episodes of hypomania were overlooked and, if even they were not dramatic, there is no law that says the first serious episode of illness has to be a manic or hypomanic episode. There are individuals who have had numerous episodes of depression without periods of significant mania or hypomania only because those episodes have not yet occurred. Almost always, mild episodes of hypomania can be discovered with careful history evaluation.

The Hyperthymic Personality

We all know the type of person who is always "on the go," volunteering for projects, leading the community, always cheerful and productive. In the hyperthymic temperament, the individual may have frequent cycles of increased energy and productivity and decreased need for sleep. Perhaps she may appear to have this high energy level as an ongoing personality trait. Although this type of personality is not really considered a bipolar disorder, it is often the forerunner, or what is known as a "premorbid personality." Unlike someone with ADHD, the hyperthymic personality is able to sustain attention, focus, complete tasks and accomplish goals.

Imagine how much you could accomplish if you required only three or four hours of sleep every night. The bulk of us who require seven or eight hours of sleep and recreational time on weekends often find ourselves tired from the demands of daily life. Raising kids, showing up for a job, taking care of the household, and trying to squeeze in a little time for community or religious activities is just about all that even the most motivated and conscientious individual can manage. There are different levels of hyperthymia, but in general we are looking at someone who is driven to create, consume, and produce. There may be different avenues for this energy. If we look at our political leaders, we find folks who can chair a seven a.m. breakfast meeting, see constituents and lobbyists throughout the day, draft legislation, attend long winded budget meetings, attend speaking engagements, and party at receptions until late in the evening. During campaign season, there are stops, meetings, and fund raisers from dawn until midnight. Most human beings simply do not have the stamina for this kind of schedule, but the avid politician thrives on this type of activity and attention. He might even describe it as his life blood. Rarely do such people seem to tire. In order to rise to a level of prominence in politics, it is necessary to have some of this extra store of energy. It is a gift(or perhaps curse) with which one is born.

When thinking of the businessman who is unstoppable, Lee Iacocca or Donald Trump come to mind. There is the buying and selling, and wheeling and dealing that are part of the game. It is not difficult to visualize Mr. Trump, dressed in suit and tie in the wee hours of the morning, on the phone making deals and money. Although Mr. Trump has more money than he ever needs to spend, it is the game, the challenge, or "The Art of the Deal" which is a powerful and seductive force.

Thomas Edison was one of the most creative and productive inventors of modern history. He could go lengthy periods of time with very little sleep, often getting by with cat naps on a cot in his laboratory. Prolific writers like James Michener or Stephen King, or highly productive artists like Picasso or Degas were not only blessed with genius, but also with that extra battery pack of energy that allowed them to express their genius in a way that would ultimately bring attention, success, and rewards well deserved.

Most of us could not write a nine hundred page novel even if we did have the creative ideas for such a time consuming enterprise in the first place. Perhaps the hyperthymic temperament is a gift bestowed on a chosen few who can then provide a wonderful combination of leadership and creativity that will guide and inspire the rest of us. There may be a positive upside to this bipolar spectrum and the downside may be just an expression of the evolution of our creative selves that has gone astray.

There are very few pure hyperthymic individuals. Even those who experience hyperthymia must often pay a price. Years of hyperthymia may appear to be the personality trait of a successful motivated person, but sooner or later, the dark downside of the cycle will appear. The first significant depressive episode may not occur until mid life. Then it seems all the more cruel since she is not really skilled in coping with depression. Sometimes hyperthymia will turn into frank mood cycling which will consistent with a bipolar II disorder. It is often inexplicable why someone who is very high functioning would all of a sudden "crash and burn" for no apparent reason.

Bipolar disorders evolve differently within each individual. Unfortunately, in American culture, deterioration from a previous level often needs to be blamed on somebody or something. For example, a very well functioning worker with a good record may find himself not being able to live up to his previous standards as he cycles down into his first significant depression. This, of course leads to decreased work performance which comes to the attention of coworkers and supervisors. The negative feedback is interpreted as harassment, and the functioning continues to deteriorate even further. The "harassment" of the workplace eventually becomes identified as the cause, not the result of the evolving disability. This leads to a workman's compensation claim with the accompanying litigation.

Another disadvantage of the hyperthymic temperament is that the driven, energetic quality that can lead to personal success can also lead to lapses in judgement. Highly energetic, successful people also tend to have an increased appetite for risky activities and sexual liaisons. There is never a shortage of sex scandals in Washington or other world capitals. Leaders who sometimes work around the clock and even on vacation, also require a fair amount of sexual release. High levels of drive and energy will not always be channeled into ways we deem socially acceptable. We sometimes do not hold our leaders to the same moral standards to which we hold ourselves and our children. Movie stars are talented, highly driven, restless people who can also be vain and narcissistic. Their multiple affairs and serial monogamy have become our cultural jokes. This leads to philosophic questions about character and personal responsibility which should be included in an overall therapeutic approach when such an individual seeks treatment.

Sometimes hyperthymia will swing out of control and move into the realm of hypomania or mania. It is at this point that the patient will come to the attention of the mental health system. The highly adaptive hyperthymic who has the trappings of success, wealth, and admiration usually will not seek or require treatment until some level of instability occurs. Most commonly this may involve some type of substance abuse. Athletes and movie stars make the news with arrests for brawls or speeding as these highly driven people move into more frank mood cycling. Proper management and treatment of the problem can restore balanced living.

Chronic Dysthymia

Some unfortunate people seem to have long histories of intermittent depression. There is such a concept as recurrent unipolar depression, but depending on the length, quality, and history of these depressions, it may be quite likely we are looking at a mild recurring bipolar depression. Individuals may have relatively brief or somewhat lengthy periods of depression throughout much of their lives. There may be intermittent depressions that are temporarily relieved by antidepressants and the patient will stop treatment and do fine for a while. Then the depression will reoccur and she will need to get back on antidepressants once again. This may go on for years until ultimately a clear cut hypomanic episode may develop. The depressions may not be serious enough to be diagnosed as a "major depression," but studies indicate that those who suffer with this type of depression also have diminished functioning in their lives in terms of social, occupational, and intimate relationships. Since the depression generally does not meet criteria for full blown depression, Dr. Akiskal has referred to this type of depression as sub-affective dysthymia or sub-syndromal dysthymia. Even though some of the criteria, but not all the criteria, for major depression are present, this type of depression or dysthymia needs to be treated. The medical treatment may include antidepressants, but also there is the awareness of subtle bipolar component to this depression.

Other Clues For Bipolar Diagnosis

The Credit Card Sign

"Tell me about your credit cards."

This question in the middle of an evaluation often evokes some self-conscious giggles. After all, why would a doctor be asking such a question? The most common answer I get when there is a strong suspicion of bipolar disorder is "we don't have them anymore."

"So why don't you have them anymore?"

"Well, we had to get rid of them."

"Why did you have to get rid of them?"

The patient or family usually go on to weave a tale of excessive and impulsive spending. The spending occurs in episodes, or shopping sprees, usually when the patient is in a hypomanic state, and involves purchases of unneeded or unused, expensive items. He feels high and energetic and wants to spend. This is not the same as chronic compulsive spending, such as living one's life in front of cable shopping channels.

Bipolar individuals may have significant ongoing financial problems as a result of episodes of irresponsible spending, and credit cards are the perfect shovel to dig a deep hole of debt. Sooner or later, bankruptcy occurs and the credit cards get tossed away. This is what I call the credit card sign, a clue to look for when trying to make a bipolar diagnosis.

Racing Thoughts

As the bipolar individual moves into a state of agitation, thoughts begin to move rapidly. This process may be intermittent at first. The patient may complain that she cannot sleep because her mind just will not shut off. Racing thoughts are not worrying thoughts or repetitive ruminations. They are more like a flurry of disconnected ideas or static. It is important to make this distinction since the racy, speedy quality of the thoughts is characteristic of bipolar disorder.

As the racing quality progresses, it will be harder to focus and concentrate. Eventually the speech pattern becomes very rapid and disconnected, making it impossible to engage in a meaningful two-way conversation. This is a distressing symptom which often leads the patient to self-treat with alcohol or other drugs which will compound the problem.

It is always useful to inquire about racing thoughts, particularly occurring at night while trying to sleep. The patient may not understand that this is an abnormal process with a name and will be quite relieved to know she is not alone with this type of symptom. Proper medication will slow down the raciness and help with sleep.

Explosive Personality Disorder

There are individuals, usually men, who are constantly getting into trouble with their temper. He may be the abusive husband, the guy with the road rage, the one who gets into barroom brawls, or the fellow in the anger management class. After an incident of violence, he is characteristically remorseful. Yet, the behavior is repeated from time to time. The experience is described as an uncontrollable urge to strike out. It is often worse when the individual is intoxicated.

Another clue in the understanding and diagnosis of bipolar disorders is the element of emotional outbursts. It is as if a lot of nervous system instability builds up and is released at once, followed by a period of depletion or remorse. There is a significant analogy to bipolar mood cycling with a release of manic energy followed by low energy or depression. This explosiveness appears to be a variation of bipolar disorder. The anticonvulsants which are useful for bipolar disorders are also useful in controlling mood outbursts. Currently Depakote is considered the drug of choice for explosive disorders just as it is for bipolar disorders. Antidepressants can worsen the situation. Antipsychotic medications such as Haldol are sedating, but otherwise do not have much effect in reducing violent behavior. Zyprexa is beginning to show some promise in curbing this behavior, especially in adolescents.

Counseling and anger management training can be useful in teaching people about warning signs and developing alternative pathways in dealing with anger. But as with bipolar disorders in general, medication and counseling combined provide the best treatment results.

Angry, emotional outbursts can occur with individuals who are developmentally disabled or brain damaged. Still, anticonvulsants are considered very effective and remain the treatment of choice for these groups of patients.

Chapter Twelve

Sleep as Treatment

Probably the most urgent problem in a worsening bipolar disorder is the marked lack of sleep that occurs. When a patient is committed to a hospital for an acute manic episode, it is almost universal that the history will indicate he has not been sleeping at all for the past several nights. A more careful analysis of the sleep pattern will show the disturbance in sleep has actually been gradually developing over several weeks or longer. It only became apparent to others when the patient was actually up at night causing a lot of commotion. During such a chaotic period, the patient is not the one complaining, it is usually the other members of the household who are kept awake. The sleep pattern was probably deteriorating weeks prior to the final call to 911, but it was gradual enough that no one thought it was of any particular significance.

Such a deteriorating sleep pattern is known as a "warning sign." If recognized and treated properly in the early stages, a severe breakdown can be avoided. This applies not only to true manic depression, but other bipolar spectrum disorders as well. The most important intervention a physician can provide to a bipolar patient who is beginning to have increasing symptoms is to get that person to sleep, even if he is going to be oversedated for a few days and has to miss work.

Providing sleep is not always easy. All too often, people try to treat themselves with alcohol or marijuana. They may not recognize they have a progressive illness. Alcohol may provide some temporary relief, but sleep induced by alcohol is characteristically fitful and disturbed. Usually there is middle of the night awakening. The shakiness and irritability of a developing episode of agitation is compounded by alcohol misuse.

Physicians have legitimate concerns about prescribing addicting sleeping pills and tranquilizers, especially if the patient has a history of "substance abuse." On the other hand we are dealing with a legitimate medical emergency, and proper treatment can prevent a crisis.

The first step in helping induce sleep is a class of medication known as benzodiazepines, affectionately known as "benzos." This is also known as the Valium family, a group of mild tranquilizers and sleeping pills. Valium, Ativan, Xanax and Klonopin are among the tranquilizing agents. The most common sleeping pills in this group are the widely used Restoril and Dalmane. Substance abuse counselors hate benzos and refer to them as "chewable alcohol" since there is a chemical relationship to alcohol and they can be similarly addicting. Still, cautious and carefully monitored usage of these medications can be very helpful with an agitated bipolar individual, even if there has been a history of substance abuse.

If sleep deterioration is more advanced, it may be necessary to add one of the antipsychotic drugs which have a significant tranquilizing effect. During this phase of treatment, it is understood that a patient will need to be on one of the mood stabilizing drugs as well.

It is most important that all antidepressant medications be stopped immediately. Sometimes during the early phase of treatment, a physician might prescribe one of the more sedating antidepressants which is, without a doubt, a big mistake. It is unfortunate but common to see someone spinning into sleepless agitation after being prescribed antidepressants that were intended to help with a sleep problem.

A patient suffering from a mixed mood state or developing mania needs to be quickly sedated. If a lot of medication is required, she may need to be in the hospital for safety and monitoring reasons. Lithium or Depakote may take days to provide symptom relief, whereas benzos or antipsychotic drugs will provide almost immediate relief.

Getting a good night's sleep early in treatment helps set up the nervous system and the rest of the body to respond to the other treatments that are to follow. Sleep alone is not the only treatment, and there is much else that needs to be done. There is certainly no reason for an irritable, agitated patient to be wandering the hallways of the hospital ward wringing her hands, crying and cursing. She needs to be asleep. Forcing her into her room because it is the rule is not useful. Proper medical treatment involves sedation and sleep. Even though family members may be concerned about the considerable sedation, it should be pointed out that this is just a temporary condition and that sedation will be reduced over the next several days. Most patients are happy with the initial sedation since this may be the first opportunity in days or weeks to not feel agitated. As they recover, the sedation is removed and they are able to return home.

There are a number of interventions beyond medication a bipolar patient can do to help maintain good sleep patterns. Good sleeping patterns, sometimes referred to as sleep hygiene, is a very important ongoing treatment which can help prevent relapses into agitated mixed states. The first step is to maintain regular sleep habits. There should be a routine time of going to bed and a routine time of rising up in the morning. It is not unusual for many of us to like to "sleep in" on weekends. Although this may be harmless on occasion, it may make it more difficult to get up Monday morning. This is almost like jet lag, with the body's rhythms thrown out of balance. That is why a regular sleep pattern should be maintained on weekends, holidays and vacations as well.

Rotating shift work is something bipolar patients should never do since they are very sensitive to disturbances in sleep patterns. If a bipolar person works in an environment where shift work is generally required, some accommodation should be made in accordance with the Americans With

Disabilities Act to allow him to work routinely on one shift, and day shift would be most desirable.

Most importantly, one must remember and pay attention to the warning signs of developing disturbances in sleep patterns. This is often the first symptom of a problem. One or two nights of difficulty may not necessarily be ominous, but if a pattern of insomnia at night and irritability by day are progressing, the treating physician should be seen immediately. Adjustment in medication may lead to the avoidance of a crisis.

Seasonal Affective Disoeder

The winter blues are related to the decreased intensity of sunlight in our environment more so than any worries we may have about the business of the holiday season. For reasons not yet completely clear, individuals with bipolar disorders seem to be more sensitive to seasonal variations to sunlight intensity. This is one of the historical clues in developing a history of bipolar disorder. Individuals with seasonal affective disorder (SAD) experience increasing depression during the times of year when sunlight is low. It starts to become noticeable in late fall and peaks in January, which may explain the high suicide rate which occurs during that month. In the southern hemisphere, SAD develops in the corresponding winter months which are June, July and August. Christmastime down under is not associated with depression since it is the beginning of the summer season.

One hypothesis as to why bipolar disorder is associated with SAD is that both disorders are associated with disturbances in normal biologic rhythms. There is a natural tendency for many people to sleep more in the winter which is a throwback to hibernation. With bipolar individuals, this may be accompanied by an overall decrease in energy and development of depression. It follows that if you routinely develop depression during the late fall and early winter, it would be wise to be evaluated for the possibility of low level bipolar depression.

Some novel treatments have been shown to be quite effective. Over the last several years, there has been an increasing popularity of what is known as a "lightbox" with high intensity full spectrum lighting which should be turned on early in the morning and kept about three feet from the face for about twenty to thirty minutes. It is recommended that usage begin in mid-autumn and continue through spring.

Melatonin is a naturally occurring hormone which also helps regulate the sleep-wake cycle. It is available in pill form and is widely used by many people as a sleep aid. It is thought to be helpful for bipolar patients with sleep disturbance, particular those who have seasonal affective disorder and is also useful to help regularize sleep patterns for those who work rotating or night shifts or who suffer from jet lag. This is particularly important for bipolar patients who must keep their sleep patterns even and regular.

More research needs to be done in this area since some recent studies have thrown some doubt on the effectiveness of melatonin. Some evidence which is called anecdotal evidence still supports the use and effectiveness of melatonin. This means that the support for its use is derived from stories and anecdotes, but such support does not stand up, at least so far, to strict scientific scrutiny.

Chapter Thirteen

What Isn't Bipolar

What They Don't Tell You About Diet Pills

Melissa is a forty-two year old woman who was brought to the emergency room by ambulance after significantly slicing up her wrists at home. She required about twenty-five stitches as she had really gone to work on both wrists which led to a rather dramatic amount of bleeding. The cutting was rather painful. She yelled out a number of times which aroused her husband who was more than shocked to see his wife sitting in the bathtub cutting herself with blood splattering everywhere. He was able to wrestle the knife away from her while she yelled and flailed her arms. Her fourteen year old son was also aroused and called 911 immediately which brought out the paramedics. Once they arrived, Melissa had to be restrained while they put emergency bandages on both wrists. She required restraint in the ambulance as well. When the arrived at the emergency room she was given an emergency injection of the major tranquilizer, Haldol which quieted her down rather quickly. Within thirty minutes she was asleep.

The emergency room physician was most curious about this. Melissa's husband, Allen, reported that she had been acting strangely over the last week or so. Before this last week, however, she never had any type of violent outburst or agitation. There was some depression and irritability which occurred during her premenstrual phase, so her family physician had prescribed Prozac for her. She had been taking this for about six months without any apparent problems. She had been sleeping well and generally eating well. She had gained about ten pounds over the previous six months since starting the Prozac and was somewhat concerned about this.

Melissa had not been sleeping for the three or four nights immediately prior to this incident. She was also noted by her family to be very irritable and snappy which was completely out of character for her. There was also some shakiness present and her husband reported she had trouble holding her coffee cup still while drinking.

The question arose of whether or not Melissa was sneaking some drugs of abuse on the sly, but her family insisted she was a good church going woman who never had anything to do with drugs and very little to do with alcohol. The routine urine drug screen taken in the emergency room that evening was negative for any types of drugs of abuse.

There was one very curious incident that had occurred two nights before. Melissa had accused her teenage son of moving things around in her closet or perhaps even removing them. There was no evidence for this and her husband, Allen, vouched for his son that there would be no reason for him to do such a thing. That same evening Melissa complained about music coming from the neighbors' house. Allen had to convince her there was no music being played, at least none he could hear.

Arrangements were made for Melissa to be transferred to the inpatient psychiatric ward on a legal hold. She was given the diagnosis of "psychosis, not otherwise specified."

When I first met Melissa the next morning, I had already read the evaluation summary prepared by the psychologist in the emergency room. Melissa was sleeping rather soundly in the unlocked seclusion room where the staff could keep an eye on her. This was uncommon in light of the rather serious nature of her suicide attempt. I was told by the staff that she had been sleeping through the entire night. The only medication she had been given was an injection of five milligrams of Haldol the night before. This apparently sedated her quite well as it appeared as though she was catching up on her sleep. I was surprised, since I expected to see a very agitated, psychotic woman. What I saw, however, was someone who was rather hard to rouse. With some encouragement she did open her sleepy eyes and was able to sit up. Both wrists were bandaged, but she was able to move her hands well enough. She swept back the matted hair from her forehead and asked that I forgive her rather unseemly appearance. She requested a few minutes to freshen up and fix herself up as well as well as clear some of the cobwebs from her head. Since this was a very reasonable request, I agreed we would meet and talk and try to figure things out in about twenty minutes. We met in the interview room after the agreed upon interval, and she seemed surprisingly calm, alert and coherent. Once she properly groomed herself, she appeared like a normal, calm, middle-aged woman without any psychiatric difficulty. The only telltale sign of problems was the bandaged wrists. She placed her forearms on her lap and looked somewhat bewildered at the wrists saying "I don't know what happened, I just don't know what came over me."

"Let's talk about it," I said. So we did.

I reviewed very carefully Melissa's history going back to childhood looking for any clues that might lead to an understanding of this emotionally charged suicide attempt. She told me she did not feel particularly depressed. The Prozac had been helpful (although she had not received it yet today). She was not taking hormones or steroids or any unusual type of medication. She had some depression and irritability during her premenstrual phase over the last several years, but she had never been suicidal or depressed to the point where she was not able to function. She was quite aware that over the last three weeks she had been getting more irritable with diminishing sleep. She felt that perhaps not getting sleep was an important factor in her agitation and irritability. She does not specifically remember taking a knife and trying to cut herself the night before. She does remember, however, that she was feeling at the end of her rope and was feeling so agitated that she felt she could not stand it anymore. "I must have been pretty desperate to do what I did."

"So what happened three weeks ago?"

"Nothing's changed, maybe I was worried about my weight going up over the last few months because I have always had a tendency to gain weight. But I was not worried about that too much anymore since my appetite has been pretty much under control since I started the diet pills."

"The diet pills?

"Yes, my doctor started giving me that new Phen-fen."

"And when was that?"

"About a month ago."

It looked like we were getting warm.

"Works pretty good, too," she added.

It looked like we had here a case of different doctors prescribing different drugs, each one not knowing what the other doctor was doing. Prozac is a drug that, as we well know, enhances serotonin. It is in a class known as Selective Serotonin Reuptake Inhibitors. (SSRI) The Phenfen combination of drugs also markedly enhances serotonin. One element has since been taken off the market because of alleged cardiac effects. Melissa was overloaded with serotonin because of the combination of these medications. Her brain went on the overload to the point where she was very agitated, irritable, and developing some mild psychotic symptoms. As it turned out, she had reported to her primary care physician (the one who prescribed the Prozac) that she was feeling some increased irritability and agitation. Knowing how it is with women who have PMS, he prescribed a mild tranquilizer as well to calm things down. But, as is often the case in the world of medicine, sometimes the right hand does not know what the left hand is doing. I told Melissa there will be no more diet pills for her. And just in case, perhaps she should try a different antidepressant as well, although the Prozac, in and of itself, was not really the problem. There are probably other patients who are perhaps taking diet pills plus an SSRI antidepressant such as Prozac without difficulty, but Melissa is a patient who was probably particularly sensitive to this combination.

Although it appeared at first glance that this was a woman who might be having a first psychotic break, one who appears to be manic, historical information revealed the problem to be something entirely different. Nonetheless, Melissa would remain in the hospital for another day just for the sake of observation and to make sure her blood pressure, which had been elevated in the emergency room, was stabilizing and that her mood and mental status were calm as well. She remained clear throughout the next twenty-four hours and was discharged to home. We did agree she should have a follow-up appointment the next week just to make sure everything was remaining calm, and fortunately, it did.

The final task was to inform the treating physicians what had happened. I contacted the primary physician by telephone who listened thoughtfully while I explained to him that the most likely problem here was a drug interaction. "Thanks for the heads up," he told me as we finished the conversation. Hopefully, he will take a longer view of overweight women with PMS. Also, the diet doctor will do a little more careful history taking to find out what other medications his patients are taking. My own lesson learned is do not assume every case that looks bipolar is actually bipolar.

Head Injuries

There are fancier ways to put this, but basically if someone falls down and whacks his head and suffers an injury, there can be sustained changes in mood and personality. There is a post concussion syndrome which may not involve any specific laboratory findings such as a positive CAT scan, but after a head injury, the victim can be very irritable and excitable and this could last for an indefinite period of time. Sometimes there are positive findings on CAT scans or MRI scans if somebody actually bothers to do one. Undiscovered head injuries are particularly common among older folks who may slip and fall and hurt themselves at home. This could also be found among street people, and drug abusers and misusers who often will have incidents of falling down and hitting their heads. Sometimes these injuries lead to rather brief periods of amnesia. So it is possible for someone to injure her head especially during an alcoholic episode and not even remember she had a head injury or blackout. An injury where someone will injure the brain without obvious skull fracture is known as a closed head injury.

This brings us to the case of Carolyn.

Carolyn had been attending the counseling clinic for about three months because of increasing agitation and irritability. She had been unable to focus on her job as a licensed practical nurse. She had been forgetting to carry out tasks, she was becoming more sensitive to stress, more irritable in mood and sometimes snapping back at supervisors. Prior to this year she had been generally a good employee with a good work record. But now she was receiving some negative feedback at work about her job performance. She said she was unable to sleep. She complained that her thoughts were racing and that her moods were very labile with frequent tearfulness. One day at the women's self-esteem (borderline) group she expressed some suicidal thoughts. The therapist in charge of the group was alarmed and spoke with Carolyn after the group. Carolyn broke down in tears and became very shaky and agitated. The therapist thought it would be best for Carolyn to be evaluated on the inpatient psychiatric unit at the hospital.

When Carolyn arrived at the hospital she discussed her symptoms of including sleeplessness, and decreased ability to focus and concentrate. She was diagnosed as having one of the bipolar spectrum disorders. Her history was carefully reviewed and, after Carolyn settled down with some medication, she gave a story of a blacking out spell she had about six or seven months prior. She denied having any kind of head injury but said she just merely passed out while crossing the street. She denied falling over and bumping her head, but stated she simply got dizzy and blacked out. She remembers that some tests had been performed, but did not exactly remember the results, though she believes she had a CAT scan in the past. Her medical records were ordered and ultimately the results of the scans were reviewed. Interestingly enough, the test showed a significant degree of bleeding in the brain which had occurred. It was not clear exactly why this happened, whether there was a stroke or a weakness in one of the vessels. She had been hospitalized in intensive care for about three days, but was discharged after it was apparent she had recovered most of her functions. She had no weakness in her arms or legs. She seemed fairly intact in terms of her ability to think and reason and do calculations. It was only after she returned to work that her decreasing ability to function on the job was noted. It was at that point she began attending the mental health clinic. She recalls she had an episode of depression about ten years prior when she had broken up with a previous boyfriend. She had been on antidepressants for about a year, but seemed to do well after they were discontinued and she went on with her life.

While attending the mental health clinic prior to her hospitalization, Carolyn had been restarted on the antidepressant desipramine which seemed to help briefly. Soon she became more irritable and agitated and was sleeping very poorly even with medication. She was asking for some sleeping medication which worked only intermittently. There were some notes from the referring therapist's file that Carolyn was observed to be "drug seeking." She had frequent emotional outbursts during group therapy and at one point there was a conference among the team members that Carolyn should be dropped from the group and perhaps even from the clinic since she was seen as being uncooperative and not responsive to treatment.

The problem was that the history of the head injury was never specifically relayed to the treatment team at the mental health center. Despite that fact, the test results were clearly delineated on the medical file. The results of the CAT scan showed a considerable amount of bleeding, although the test itself did not reveal the reason for this.

Carolyn's symptoms appeared to be very consistent with mood instability. However, this was not due to any underlying primary bipolar disorder but was secondary to head injury.

There are reasons why the treatment team could be fooled with Carolyn. First of all, she had been previously diagnosed as having depression years before, and in the realm of psychiatry, once an individual receives a diagnosis, it tends to stay with her for life. In this case, she was seen as an individual with possible recurring depression. Also, she was in the age range where the onset of bipolar disorder could be considered, although onset is more common at a younger age. Since she had a depression at age twenty-five, this might have been considered "younger age." However, the treatment team was looking more at the diagnosis of personality disorder than a bipolar disorder. Also, since Carolyn was female, and presented as somewhat unstable, team members relegated her to the diagnostic wastebasket of borderline personality disorder.

There should also be a good amount of suspicion when an elderly individual develops what is thought to be manic depression. It is not outside the realm of possibility that bipolar disorder can develop in later life, but it is quite unusual and should be looked at with a significant degree of suspicion.

Little Strokes

Henry is a seventy-four year old man who was first diagnosed as having a bipolar disorder at age seventy. He is a retired postal worker who lives with his wife. Prior to age seventy he had no psychiatric diagnosis or problems whatsoever. About four years prior to his hospitalization he was noted to be more irritable, not sleeping at night, quite moody, sometimes had trouble focusing, sometimes he would lose his temper rather easily. He did not seem to have particular problems with depression, although there were times when his wife noted he was quite withdrawn and was worried he may have a serious depression. On one or two occasions he had talked about "ending it all" but, when questioned by an evaluating psychiatrist at the mental health center, he stated he just gets frustrated and irritated at times and he really was not suicidal. Indeed, he had never made any type of suicide attempt and never had any plans. However, he had seemed to lose interest in some of the things he enjoyed and did not seem as interested in spending time with his grandchildren or watching sports on television, which were two of his favorite activities.

Henry had been started on lithium and a low dose of antidepressant and seemed to do somewhat better and was a little calmer. He still had some problems sleeping at night and was often up early in the morning. Yet he was able to participate in family activities and although he was not doing overall as well as he used to, his mood seemed to be stabilizing. There was a little confusion at times. He could not remember what time certain television shows were on and sometimes complained he could not remember what he had for breakfast or was asking his wife for lunch when he had just had it an hour before.

One day while his daughter and grandson were visiting, Henry became very irritable. For a while it seemed as though he was confused, groping for words, unable to concentrate. His wife had later noted he had not been sleeping well for the last three nights. He was starting to use foul language in front of the grandchild and threw a shoe across the room, but not at anybody in particular. Later that same day he started breaking things and had to be restrained. He was taken to the emergency room by his family where he was placed on a legal hold for being acutely manic. He was evaluated by the consulting psychologist in the Emergency Room who saw the patient as being confused and very agitated.

Henry was paranoid, accusing people of laughing at him and stealing his things. He was pacing, restless. He knew the date but thought he was in jail. Henry had a lithium level of 0.4 which is considered a little lower than the minimum therapeutic level. He had also been on a low dose of the mild tranquilizer clonazepam but no level was measured. The psychologist recommended that Henry be transferred to the psychiatric ward where his "anti-manic depression medication can be stabilized."

When Henry arrived at the psychiatric ward, it was apparent he was not going to follow directions very readily since he was threatening and unccooperative, and, on one or two occasions, seemed to want to strike out at staff who were coming close to him. The alert charge nurse was able to calm Henry down and, with some quick physical evaluation, was able to determine that Henry had significant problems moving his right arm and right leg and that he had probably had a recent stroke. Henry was transferred from the psychiatric ward to the emergency room where he was further evaluated by a neurologist. Diagnostic studies including an MRI scan of the brain revealed numerous small lesions consistent with what are known as "micro infarcts" and a larger, more recent area of bleeding. Micro infarcts are essentially very tiny areas of brain tissue which degenerate after the blood supply is diminished or cut off because of diminished circulation.

In reconstructing Henry's case history, it seems not likely that Henry developed bipolar disorder at age seventy, but that he was experiencing changes in his behavior and mood secondary to a diminishing blood flow to various regions of his brain. Although he was not having any physical weakness, there was clear cut irritability, sleep disturbances, and some losses in his ability to think clearly. It certainly would have been useful for Henry to have received some type of diagnostic CAT scan or MRI scan four years ago when his symptoms started to become apparent rather than making assumptions about his clinical presentation based on incomplete information.

The above cases of Carolyn and Henry illustrate the onset of a presentation of what may appear to be a bipolar disorder when what is really going on is some underlying brain pathology. In both cases the brain problems were secondary to circulation problems. Any elderly individual with a change in personality and mood requires evaluation with a great deal of suspicion.

It is also known that injury to the brain through concussion such as what occurs during a football game, a boxing match or perhaps an automobile accident or fall can lead to changes in behavior as well. Although bipolar disorder is generally diagnosed on the basis of a complete and thorough history taken by the clinician, head injuries followed by changes in behavior, even if they appear to be bipolar in nature, need to be further evaluated with brain studies and psychological testing to define any impairment in intelligence and reasoning that may occur in the long run.

Antidepressant Blues

Every time antidepressants seem to make a situation worse, it may be something other than a bipolar patient responding poorly to antidepressant as can be seen in the following example.

Tony is a fifty-one year old man who has had some intermittent depression through his life. He developed a rather serious depression about two years ago when he was divorced. Up until that time he had been working as a software engineer in a company that was downsizing. He was fearful of losing his job but, because of his specialized skills, he had a relatively safe position. Unfortunately, his work demands increased as other workers were laid off. The combination of stressors led Tony to become depressed and his family physician started him on an SSRI antidepressant. His mood seemed to pick up a little bit, and his energy improved, but after about two or three months he became more lethargic and was unable to get through the workday. He complained about being tired. His family physician referred him to a psychiatrist who felt, since the antidepressant was at least somewhat helpful, perhaps a combination with a second type of antidepressant might augment the effect of the first one. This is a technique commonly used. Very often individuals with depression end up on two antidepressants and sometimes even other drugs in combination.

Unfortunately, Tony did not seem to improve and remained very listless and withdrawn. He felt something was wrong with him physically. Tony complained he was quite tired and was now sleeping twelve to fourteen hours a day. He was not feeling particularly depressed and he no longer had any type of suicidal ideas. He was not even feeling agitated, just very tired and withdrawn. He was now on disability leave from work and was very concerned about his job being available when he returned, if indeed he ever would be able to return to work. His appetite was not bad. As a matter of fact, he had gained a few pounds since this lethargy started. His psychiatrist was thinking perhaps there may be some type of medical illness, perhaps a chronic viral infection or chronic fatigue syndrome. Laboratory tests are generally not very helpful. So far, we know chronic fatigue syndrome is associated with depression and it was thought that this was the case with Tony.

In reviewing his history, Tony had been on five different antidepressants including the two he was currently taking. There was some sense that he should try an "energizing" antidepressant, but the various switches did not provide much benefit.

Sometimes when nothing seems to be working, physicians will withdraw all the medications for a "washout" to see how the patient does on nothing at all. The antidepressants were tapered and discontinued. Tony's lethargy diminished and his energy returned to near normal within two weeks. Why did stopping the antidepressants lead to an improvement in his energy level? We know that antidepressants can sometimes be sedating and sometimes they can be energizing. This level of lethargy is quite uncommon. What happened with Tony is an occasional side effect of antidepressants which is only compounded when the antidepressants are increased or combined with others. The lethargy and withdrawal involve dopamine depletion which can occur with antidepressants. Antidepressants can enhance some chemicals of the brain at the expense of others. Medications which enhance dopamine activity often counteract this lethargic response. There are some drugs that are not generally well known such as Parlodel and Amantadine which can counteract this effect. Also, dopamine enhancing antidepressants such as venlafaxine can also be useful in counteracting this effect.

The example of Tony illustrates a case where antidepressants actually did seem to be make someone worse, but not in the context of a bipolar disorder. It may have been tempting to add a drug like lithium or Depakote, but in a case like this, it would have been more useful to add a dopamine enhancing drug. In this case, removing the antidepressants was also useful, although whether or not Tony needs to return to an antidepressant remains to be seen. His psychiatrist opted to wait things out, figuring that in terms of medication for Tony "less is more."

By the way, Tony did not have at worry about losing his job since he worked for a company large enough that it was affected by the Americans With Disabilities Act and the Family Leave Act, so he was able to take up to ninety days leave time without fearing loss of his employment. Fortunately, Tony had an understanding employer who would have allowed him to have even more time off if necessary.

Tony continued in ongoing therapy on a weekly basis which seemed to be helpful and, ultimately, he was able to get by without any psychiatric medication.

Chapter Fourteen

Thr Antimanic Drugs

Lithium

Lithium is one of the most written about medications in the world. There are many informative books for physicians as well as for the public which describe the use of lithium, its properties and therapeutic effects.

What Is Lithium?

Lithium is a basic element found in the earth's crust. If you ever had a basic chemistry course, perhaps you remember what was known as the Periodic Table of the Elements. The elements are arranged from the lightest to the heaviest with hydrogen being the very lightest and helium being the next lightest and number three on the list is lithium which is the lightest of the solid elements. It is actually considered a metal. It has some commercial uses beyond being used as a drug. For example, it is used in the manufacture of rechargeable batteries. In the early 1940s it was used to help reduce swelling and edema and was found to be a useful diuretic.

Early researchers noticed that it helped stabilize mood and reduce mania. In the 1940s and 1950s, researchers such as Cade in Australia and Mogens Schou in Denmark produced massive amounts of research proving its usefulness in reducing and alleviating manic symptoms. Although widely used in Europe during the 1950s and 1960s, it was not approved for use in the United States until 1970. Acceptance was slow, and this was related to the common problem of misdiagnosis of manic depression in this country. Through the 1970s and perhaps even through today, many frank manic depressive individuals are still diagnosed as schizophrenic. Although medications such as Haldol, Thorazine, Navane and Stelazine can calm a manic patient rather quickly, it takes lithium several days to become effective, so it is not unusual for a patient who is having a manic episode of psychotic proportions to be placed on several medications while the lithium takes effect.

Lithium has been considered a miracle drug to clinicians who have prescribed it and studied it. Not only is lithium used for quelling acute manic episodes, it also has a very good protective function in keeping manic episodes from recurring. This is why it is essential for people with severe manic depressive illness to remain on medication even after the episodes are long past.

What Lithium Is Good For

As noted above, lithium is very useful for the treatment of acute manic episodes. It is also extremely useful in treating non-bipolar, that is, unipolar depressions by being used in combination with standard antidepressants. Although lithium alone is not considered to be a good antidepressant medication, it can be absolutely terrific when combined with antidepressants to help lift someone out of deep depression. Lithium alone, however, is much more effective at preventing recurrence of serious depression with or without the use of other antidepressants. Extensive research studies have shown that lithium is very useful for reducing the risk of suicide in depressed individuals when used on an ongoing basis. Even though some of the other mood stabilizing medications may be more effective in the short term, none of the other medications can live up to the achievement of lithium in the prevention of recurring depressions and suicide attempts.

What Lithium Is Not Good For

Lithium is not particularly useful when used alone as an antidepressant. It may have some effect over time, but it is usually not dramatic and generally not very quick. It is better used as a "booster" for other antidepressant medications.

Likewise, although lithium is good for bipolar I disorders, that is, overt manic depression particularly the manic phase, it is not nearly as useful for the more subtle types of bipolar spectrum disorders which are discussed in this book. This is particularly true for the rapid mood cyclers, that is, those individuals whose moods go up and down rather quickly in a matter of days as opposed to periods of months as seen in basic manic depression. Perhaps this is one of the reasons why the mental health professionals are slow to accept and catch on to the concept of bipolar spectrum disorders. Patients who may have episodes of mild hypomania, depression and irritability do not respond particularly well to lithium and, therefore, the diagnosis of bipolar disorder is dismissed. The other anticonvulsants, particularly Depakote, are shown to be more effective in dealing with these rapid mood cycling disorders.

Side Effects of Lithium

Practically every medication prescribed in any field of medicine has effects that are undesirable and not intended. Lithium is no exception. When discussing the need for medication, a thorough physician will discuss the risks and benefits of a medication in order to help the patient make an informed decision about whether or not to take it. Generally speaking, a medication will be prescribed only when the benefits are presumed to outweigh the risks.

Lithium is considered a safe medication but problems can and do arise.

Most common are the gastrointestinal side effects which involve upset stomach, nausea and diarrhea. A lot of people have some mild symptoms that usually abate after a few days or weeks of usage. These symptoms can be minimized by making sure the lithium is taken on a full stomach. There are some brands of lithium which have coated tablets on them which help reduce the stomach irritation. Such brands include Lithobid and Eskalith.

It is not unusual to get a little bit of shakiness, particularly a very fine tremor of the hands and finger tips. This side effect can often be eliminated by reducing the dose or making sure the patient remains well hydrated, taking plenty of fluids throughout the day. If the symptoms persist, it is important to see the prescribing physician and obtain a blood test to find out what the lithium level is in the blood and adjust the dosage accordingly.

Weight gain is an unfortunate side effect. It is probably the one problem that causes people to stop taking the medication more than any other. There are several reasons why people gain weight on lithium. The first reason is that when people are manic or very depressed, they feel poorly and do not eat well. By feeling normal again, the appetite will often increase. Also, people can be somewhat hyper and jittery prior to taking lithium. If you have ever seen someone who is a little irritable and agitated sitting jiggling their knees, tapping their pencils, standing up walking around, etc., it is easy to see that such people burn up a lot of calories which they stop doing once their physical activity settles down. Keep in mind that hyper people, more often than not, are skinny people.

Lithium is well known to slow down the thyroid gland. Although this is not a dangerous side effect, it can be annoying. As long as lithium levels are being checked, it is a good idea also to check thyroid hormone levels. Slowing down of the thyroid can be easily corrected with small doses of thyroid hormone given along with the lithium.

Another reason for weight gain is the retention of fluid which sometimes occurs with lithium. Although it has a diuretic quality, that is, it increases urination and drains off fluid from the body, it has the opposite effect with some people and causes significant fluid retention. This is a tricky symptom to treat since diuretics, i.e., "water pills," must be used very cautiously with lithium. However, a skillful physician can manage this sometimes unpleasant side effect.

Related to this fluid retention problem is the issue of having to urinate excessively. This is also a very manageable side effect which sometimes can be alleviated simply by stopping the lithium and restarting it a few days later. Because of increased urination sometimes people become very thirsty and will drink a lot of fluids throughout the day. If it is water, it turns out to be a good way to deal with the problem, but sometimes people will be drinking sodas, orange juice or milk which is another reason they will gain weight on lithium.

Creative and talented people often do their best work when in a hypomanic or hyperthymic phase. Lithium will often flatten out these activated mood states. Creative individuals such as musicians, artists and writers will often stop taking their mood stabilizing medications because they do not like the edge taken off their creativity.

There are rare reported cases of kidney and heart problems occurring with lithium. Serious problems can almost always be avoided by the monitoring of some simple laboratory tests a few times a year.

The patient and physician together must decide whether or not the benefits of taking lithium, or for that matter any medication, outweigh the risks and potential side effects and harm. This is a decision that must be made carefully, but always keeping in mind that generally lithium is quite safe and well tolerated with most people most of the time. Part of the assessment, of course, is the risk of not taking the medication and the continued risk of serious episodes and overall deterioration of life functioning.

There are significant concerns about taking lithium during pregnancy. It is known that there is a slight risk of the infant developing a serious cardiac condition known as Ebstein's Anomaly, if lithium is taken during the first trimester of pregnancy. It is a small risk, a fraction of one percent, but it is a risk. Sometimes, if a woman has a severe history of bipolar disorder, it may be prudent to continue lithium during pregnancy with careful monitoring and oversight by a psychiatrist and obstetrician. There are other risks which may occur as well, and any decision about this or any medication during pregnancy must be made in careful consultation with your treating psychiatrist and other treating physicians.

Depakote

When most people look up information about medications, they may not pay much attention the date of the reference. In references dated before 1995 or 1996, Depakote is listed strictly as an anticonvulsant medication. Despite this, Depakote has been used in the treatment of bipolar disorders for at least the past decade. However, in October 1995 the United States Food and Drug Administration (FDA) finally approved Depakote for its use in bipolar disorder.

Prior to that time, very anxious relatives of the patient receiving the medication would look up some information about the drug in a reference such as the Physician's Desk Reference (PDR) or a nursing manual and see that it is an anticonvulsant. They would angrily accompany the patient into the doctor's office demanding to know why an individual who is suffering from depression or agitation was being put on an anticonvulsant when, after all, they were not really suffering from seizures. Explanations about how an anticonvulsant can also be used as an antimanic depressive drug did not seem to provide much in the way of comfort for distressed relatives thinking perhaps this was some type of bizarre experiment.

For years, the psychiatric literature has been touting the use of anticonvulsants for bipolar disorder and, in certain cases, these have been found even to be superior to lithium. Keep in mind that once a drug is legal to be prescribed for one purpose, it is perfectly legal to prescribe it for other purposes, especially if there is research to document its effectiveness. The FDA approval makes it legal for the drug manufacturer to advertise a drug as being useful for a certain purpose.

For example: The anti-hypertensive drug Minoxidal was used to help grow hair on balding men. It was not until the late 1980s that the FDA approved it for use as a hair growth drug known as Rogaine.

The same holds true for Depakote. Depakote has been approved as an anticonvulsant for many years. However, psychiatric literature throughout the 1980s and early 1990s showed real benefit from Depakote in the treatment of certain types of mood cycling disorders. With the recent FDA approval of Depakote for use in bipolar disorders, the drug manufacturer, Abbott, can actually advertise the benefit for its use in bipolar disorder. Current references will indicate that Depakote is now used for manic depressive illness and for other bipolar forms as well. Up until quite recently when people thought of medication for use in manic depression, lithium would be the first drug to come to mind. So the question would be why do we need a drug such as Depakote?

Certainly some people cannot tolerate lithium and its side effects. But the main reason Depakote is used as a treatment in bipolar disorders is that it can be more effective than lithium for certain types of disorders. Information developed from research in recent years shows that Depakote is really quite effective for rapid cycling bipolar disorders and other bipolar spectrum disorders. It may be significantly more useful than lithium, which is not always useful for certain soft bipolar disorders. When the diagnosis of the bipolar II disorder was becoming more common, a lot of patients were placed on lithium but did not seem to improve in their mood cycling. This led the patients' families and practitioners to come to the conclusion that maybe the diagnosis was not right in the first place and perhaps lithium would not be useful and the diagnosis of bipolar II itself was not particularly useful. With the advent of the use of Depakote, however, it was found that a lot of people who suffered with mood cycling began to improve rather rapidly.

It would not be unusual for a patient to come to my office complaining of irritability, agitation, depression and not responding to other treatments including lithium. Once she was started on Depakote, it would often be the case that the individual would calm down rather rapidly, perhaps even within twenty-four to forty-eight hours. However, another interesting phenomenon would become apparent. Although the patient was calmer, she might begin to complain of feeling more depressed or more tearful. Perhaps the problem was not so much depression as sadness. Patients would begin to note they were more tearful and weepy than they were prior to going on the medication. This type of report became more the rule than the exception. It seems Depakote would be very good at knocking out the agitation within the first few days, leaving the lingering depression to become the most prominent symptom. Also, since patients are becoming less agitated, irritable, and distractable, they may be able to focus more on their actual problems. When other agitation is pulled out of the picture, the patient then becomes more aware of feelings and sadness and perhaps even depression. However, the risk of suicide becomes less, because the suicidal state occurs largely when the patient is agitated and irritable. It seems one can live better with honest feelings of sadness than an irritable, agitated depression.

Another benefit of this medication is that patients who take it begin to sleep better fairly quickly. This is especially useful in individuals who are mood cycling who have become very agitated and may go several nights with minimal or no sleep. The sleep itself is very helpful and healing.

One unfortunate side effect of Depakote is weight gain. This occurs in a majority of patients, particularly women. Weight gain is not inevitable, but some people have an extremely difficult time controlling their appetite once they are on Depakote. It is not only an issue of appetite stimulation, but the fact that people who have been fidgeting and jumping around for weeks, months, or years are now not burning up so many calories and may be gaining weight just on that basis. Also, there appears to be a direct slowing of body metabolism. Usually there is an early period of weight gain which levels off, although this may be up to thirty pounds or more. Individuals who are really committed to not gaining weight still have a difficult time maintaining reasonable body weight. For better or worse, people who do gain weight on this medication are often the same people who improve and have experience much relief from their suffering. There are some newer drugs becoming available such as Neurontin, Lamotrigene, and Topamax, which may not cause the weight gain of Depakote. However, Depakote is very effective and still remains the drug of first choice for treating people with rapidly cycling mood disorders.

Depakote is actually divalproex sodium which is a salt form of valproic acid. When I am asked to explain more about this medicine, I am often misunderstood. When told this is a salt of some form, the listener may mistakenly ask if indeed this is just a problem of not using enough salt on his food. People sophisticated in chemistry may understand the notion that we are not talking about table salt. Keep in mind that lithium carbonate is also a salt. The acid form, which is known as valproic acid, is really the so-called active form in Depakote. Again the term acid seems to raise some eyebrows and no one needs to worry about some type of acid burning a hole in his stomach. Aspirin, vitamin C and soft drinks are generally some form of acid as well. Actually, one can take valproic acid directly in the form of a drug known as Depakene, but most physicians and patients find that Depakote, the salt form of the medication is more well tolerated and causes less stomach acid.

How Much For How Long?

Everybody wants to know how long he or she is going to be taking medication, and how much. For Depakote, the basic rule is to take body weight and multiply that by ten and that is how many milligrams of Depakote is a target dose. A one hundred pound woman would probably do best on 1000 mg of Depakote taken in divided doses. That is just a guide and some people will be on more and some on less. The real way to find out how much is the right dose is by obtaining a blood test after taking the medication for five days to a week. If, however, there is improvement and there are no significant side effects, then one is probably close to the right dose. Some people do quite well on significantly less than the amount of medication calculated from this formula of body weight times ten. It is not usual for a patient to exclaim "1000 mg,...whoa! That's an awful lot, isn't it?" It may seem like a lot, but when taking headache medicine, for example, extra strength Tylenol is 500 milligrams. Every drug has its different milligram value for dosage and so it is difficult to compare one drug to another. Depakote is unique in that the maximum dosage can be started from day one. The pills usually come in 250 and 500 mg sizes and they do appear to be rather large, but most people can break them in half and take them fairly easily. The dose has to be adjusted up or down over the course of several weeks. Some people become really quite knocked out on just a small dose and others seem to be waiting for any kind of effect on rather large doses. It is simply a matter of individual metabolism. When treating a patient in the hospital, it will be very likely he will be started on a high dose. Outpatients are started at half the target dose since initially it is not uncommon to become sleepy or groggy and this causes a lot of anxiety for people at home. Usually the sleepiness, drowsiness and drugged feeling goes away, but it may recur if the dose is increased.

For lithium, Depakote, and Tegretol, blood tests are required to make sure the amount is just right and that some other chemical effects are not causing a problem. Liver enzymes often become a little elevated while taking Depakote or Tegretol. This is quite benign. However, if there are changes, then the physician needs to continue to monitor this until everything becomes stable. Sometimes liver enzymes really jump up fairly high causing alarm to physician and patient alike. But if the medication is really working well, it pays to wait this out and keep following the blood levels and liver enzyme levels. Once in a while this medication has to be discontinued simply because of some chemical reactions that occur, but this is fairly unusual. On rare occasions, anticonvulsants will drop white blood cell counts as well.

Usually all lab tests are performed at one time. It is important to remember to not take the medication the morning of the blood test. It should be about twelve hours after the nighttime dose. For example, if the medication is taken at 8:00 p.m., the blood test should be performed at 8:00 a.m. If the morning dose is taken before the blood test, it will throw the test result out of kilter and make the interpretation not very useful at all.

Usually Depakote is taken twice a day. However, if the morning dose is forgotten, one can easily double up the evening dose without any particular problem. Most people do not have too much in the way of side effects other than the weight gain noted above. Some people may have a little bit of nausea, vomiting or diarrhea. This is often transitory, but there is a small but notable percentage of individuals who will develop real stomach or bowel problems with this medication and then it has to be discontinued. Early in the course of treatment it can be stopped fairly quickly without any real problem with withdrawal. The problem of feeling drugged or drowsy can be reduced by lowering the daily dosage. However, if it persists, this may not be the medication for you.

The other question is how long one needs to be on the medication for bipolar disorder. It depends on the nature of the cycling, the intensity of the illness and how long the illness has been present. This issue really does not apply strictly to Depakote but to the other medical treatments for bipolar or mood cycling disorders as well. Anyone who has had significant cycling throughout his life will probably need to stay on the medication indefinitely which could mean forever. Unfortunately, many mood cyclers cannot be maintained on anticonvulsants or lithium alone, but occasionally an antidepressant may need to be temporarily added to the mix. Sometimes medications known as neuroleptics or major tranquilizers need to be added as well, and these are discussed under their own heading. All too often when people are feeling well they will stop taking their medication. If there has been a history of severe mood cycling in the past, it will almost always recur and be more difficult to treat the next time around. Staying on medication greatly reduces the risk of relapse. This is discussed further in the section on relapse and kindling.

The question often arises as to why anticonvulsants are good for mood cycling disorders. It is strictly theoretical, but it is possible that mood cycling is a variant of seizure disorder. In other words, instead of the body having seizures, it may very well be "emotions" which are having some type of seizure which is related to neurotransmitters and instability of neuronal membranes. Depakote can also be quite useful for behavior characterized by explosive outbursts, which an individual may feel are far beyond his control. Sometimes explosive tantrums can have an almost seizure like quality. These are well treated and often relieved by using the anticonvulsants

Tegretol (Carbamazepine)

Tegretol is the best known trade name for the anticonvulsant carbamazepine. This is an anticonvulsant that has been in use for at least the past two decades. It has been considered to be useful in combination with lithium for reducing mood cycling disorders. Carbamazepine has been shown to be probably more effective than lithium for use in controlling rapid mood cycles. However, Depakote is now considered to be the most useful drug for rapid mood cycling. Nonetheless, Tegretol has many of the same beneficial uses as Depakote. It is helpful for controlling intermittent explosive outbursts and rapid mood cycling. It has not be approved by the FDA for use in bipolar disorders and manic episodes, but this is still an accepted use in the psychiatric profession and can be considered one of the drugs which are consistent with a proper standard of care for mood cycling disorders.

Tegretol has been shown to be useful in the behavioral management of individuals with poor impulse control including developmentally disabled patients. It can be used alone or added to other mood stabilizers such as lithium or Neurontin.

One of the advantages of Tegretol is that it does not cause nearly the amount of weight gain that is experienced by some individuals who take Depakote or lithium. It is also quite sedating which may be an advantage early on in treatment when a person may be very agitated and not sleeping well. The early sedating side effects are quite significant and may be considered an actual advantage at times. The sedation side effect wears off over the course of several weeks.

Tegretol is also more likely to be more useful in the treatment of the bipolar spectrum disorders and rapid mood cycling than is lithium.

On the downside, Tegretol has been implicated in a rather rare but serious side effect which involves bone marrow suppression. This could lead to a shutdown of the blood making organ of the body and cause a severe or potentially fatal condition known as aplastic anemia. Simple blood tests early in the course of treatment usually can substantially reduce the risk of this occurring. This complication is much more rare than previously thought.

Also, Tegretol causes the type of side effects one might see with antihistamines such as dry mouth, blurring of vision, or constipation. Usually these side effects are quite manageable and reversible, meaning these symptoms will go away when the medication is stopped or reduced.

Tegretol also is involved in a lot of drug interactions. Therefore, one must be careful when prescribing or taking Tegretol in the presence of other medications. Tegretol and Depakote are sometimes given together when each of these medications is partially effective when taken alone. Many medications are metabolized and deactivated by the liver. The liver, in response to a medication present in the blood stream, will manufacture enzymes to take that substance out of the blood stream. Tegretol is very active in creating these enzymes, more so than most other drugs. What happens is that these enzymes may metabolize or "eat up" other medications in the body rendering them much less active than expected. This community of enzymes is known as the cytochrome system. Tegretol, taken along with Depakote, may activate this cytochrome system to the extent that the Depakote level in the blood may become quite low despite the fact that large doses are being taken. Suspicious physicians may suspect the patient is not really taking the medications as directed, but the real culprit is the nature of the interactions of the drugs being taken. However, Tegretol will not lower the levels of medications such as lithium or Neurontin since both those medications are processed by the kidney and not the liver.

Verapamil

Verapamil is best known by the trade name of Calan. It is a special type of anticonvulsant known as a calcium channel blocker. Although sometimes used as an anticonvulsant, it is also used as a high blood pressure medication. It has also been used for a certain type of vascular headache such as migraine or cluster headaches. There have been studies indicating that Verapamil may be useful in helping to control mood cycling disorders, particularly in combination with other anticonvulsant drugs. The jury is still out on Verapamil. With the new anticonvulsants available, it is not considered a particularly good choice for dealing with disorders of mood.

Topamax (Topirimate)

There is some gradually developing evidence suggesting this new anticonvulsant is useful for mood cycling disorder. There has been some anecdotal evidence that it is useful for controlling severe mood cycling disorders that have not responded to other mood stabilizers. More strict scientific studies are underway. There is a lot of excitement about this new anticonvulsant, since early reports suggest it does not only not cause weight gain, but has been shown to cause some weight loss as well. I have used it on a few overweight patients who have not responded well to other mood stabilizing drugs. So far they seem stable and they have been losing weight. However, because of the lack of research data, it is most prudent not to use this as a drug of first choice at this point, despite the abundance of patients who desire it.

Use of Topamax should not be considered lightly since it can have important side effects, particularly, significant sedation, dizziness, and on rare occasion, kidney stones.

Dilantin (Phenytoin)

Dilantin has been the most common anticonvulsant and has been around for a long time. Most people are familiar with the use of Dilantin in epilepsy. Over the years Dilantin has been touted as not only being a terrific anticonvulsant, but also useful for many maladies from depression to hemorrhoids and everything in between. Most of these claims have not been borne out, although Dilantin is still widely used for seizures. It has not been shown to be useful in treating mood cycling disorders.

Lamictal (Lamotrigene)

Lamictal became available in 1997 and is also a promising anticonvulsant with some very good success at controlling mood cycling symptoms. It appeared to be better than some of the other anticonvulsant medications. One of the benefits of Lamictal is that it seems not to cause much in the way of weight gain at all and even weight loss in a number of patients. Once in a while, patients will have a "mood switch" with Lamictal which means, if a patient starts on it when seriously depressed, her mood may "switch" to somewhat of a hyperactive or even a euphoric mood within a few days. Unless the individual becomes overtly manic, it is not necessary to stop the medication, but perhaps to just add some other medications to reduce the overactivity. Generally, this hyper mood state will resolve within a few days. Another downside of Lamictal is the occasional (less than one percent) occurrence of a syndrome which involves development of a severe rash which may actually cause the skin to fall off if it progresses far enough. The allergic reaction may eventually affect internal organs as well and could conceivably cause death. Although ten to fifteen percent of people taking Lamictal will develop a rash, less than one percent really have the type of rash that progresses into the dangerous syndrome. No matter what, it is a good idea to discontinue the medication if any kind of rash develops and discuss it with your prescribing physician. To minimize the rash risk, the dosage has to be started fairly low and increased very slowly. For example, most individuals will start on Lamictal 50 mg at bedtime and must remain on this dose for two weeks until it can be increased to 50 mg twice a day. Another two weeks has to pass prior to raising the dose any further. If a rash has not developed, then the dosage can be increased a little more rapidly. This means it takes at least four weeks to really start getting the dose up to therapeutic level for most people, although a lot of people respond very well to the lower dosages of 75 to 100 mg a day.

Despite the risk of the severe rash developing which resembles a medical syndrome known as Stevens-Johnson Syndrome, the problems for the most part can be avoided if the medication is withdrawn at the immediate onset of a rash. When used in combination with Depakote, the risk of a rash is higher because there is a drug interaction with Depakote which would cause the blood level of the Lamictal to be higher. Therefore, the dose must be lower when used in combination with Depakote, although some authorities recommend not mixing these two drugs. Lamictal can be used safely with many other mood stabilizing and antidepressant drugs.

Neurontin (Gabapentin)

Neurontin is one of the anticonvulsant mood stabilizers that has come into common usage in recent years. Originally, it was used as an "add on" anticonvulsant with other anti-epileptic drugs in individuals who were not achieving good seizure control. As most of the other anticonvulsants, it has not been formally approved for use in mood cycling disorders, yet controlled studies have been finding it useful in stabilizing mood. Overall, it is milder than some of the antimanic drugs and may not be particularly useful in treating acute manic episodes when used alone. It has fewer side effects than a lot of other anticonvulsants, although early in treatment it can cause quite a bit of sedation so it has to be started at a low dose. The starting dose is at 300 milligrams, usually at bedtime and then this increases to 300 mg twice a day. Very often the dose is increased up to 1800 mg a day or more. Since it is cleared out of the body by the kidneys instead of the liver, there are not a lot of drug interactions to worry about. Although weight gain can occur with Neurontin, it does not seem as frequent or severe as with many of the other medications prescribed for bipolar disorder. Although I have seen a few patients gain considerable weight with Neurontin, I have also seen patients lose weight with it even if they gained weight with Depakote.

Neurontin is now proving useful in the treatment of chronic pain conditions, although it may take several weeks for it to become effective. Also, it is becoming more favored as a medication for anxiety without being addictive. More research needs to be done, but it appears Neurontin will have several beneficial uses in the field of psychiatry.

Chapter Fifteen

The Major Tranquilizers

The term for this type of medication changes since there are certain emotional and political stigma attached to the use of these drugs. Sometimes they are called neuroleptics based on their effect on the nervous system. Then there is the more straightforward name, "antischizophrenic" drug which sends any potential recipient of such medication running for cover. The same holds true of the term "antipsychotic drug." Also, there is the more neutral label of "phenothiazine" which, to be chemically correct, refers only to a small number of these drugs, but the name still sticks when applied to the entire group of these medications. While it is true this category of medications is indeed used to treat schizophrenia and other severe psychotic disorders, they are also used to treat a wide variety of other problems and generally in more modest doses than would be used for a full blown psychosis.

Between the early 1950s and 1990, there was very little change in the effectiveness of these so called major tranquilizers, although slightly different formulations were created by each of the major drug companies so as to be able to get a hold on this lucrative market. Some of these medications include the original phenothiazines which are Thorazine, Mellaril, and Stelazine. Then along came Haldol, Navane, Prolixin, and Loxitane which are chemically a little different and, therefore, technically not phenothiazines but still have essentially the same effect. When the first of these medications came along in the early to mid 1950s, a substantial difference was made in the treatment of chronic schizophrenic patients. In the 1960s, state mental institutions began to open their doors and allow severely mentally ill patients to be treated at local mental health clinics and, to a large part, return to the community. Not all patients respond well to these medications and many who do develop significant side effects including stiffness and tremors and a shuffling gait variously known as the "Thorazine shuffle" or "Haldol shuffle." These symptoms look very much like Parkinson's Disease and actually affect the brain in such a way as to cause the mimicking of Parkinsonism.

Long term usage of these medications commonly leads to another side effect known as tardive dyskinesia or "TD" which involves all types of tics, odd movements, and grimaces which are difficult to control.. These symptoms often look like some type of mental illness in and of itself, but actually were the result of long term use of these medications. Chronic mental patients who did not respond to one of these medications might be tried on another one, but that would rarely be useful since all these medications worked on the same specific neurotransmitter locations in the brain. With the release of Clozaril in 1990, an entirely different mechanism of dealing with psychosis was now being utilized. The Parkinson like side effects were no longer common, and the patients who never responded well to the other medications were now beginning to respond very well to this new medication.

However, Clozaril had the unfortunate side effect of causing collapse of the bone marrow with decreased immune functioning in perhaps one percent of patients. As it turned out, anyone who was taking Clozaril had to have a blood test every week to make sure the blood cells were intact. There was also the problem of expense, in that Clozaril costs thousands of dollars a year to take, not even counting the expense of the blood tests.

Clozaril was the first of what was called the "novel antipsychotics." That is, it worked a different way than the whole batch of antipsychotics worked prior to 1990. Now there is increased hope for clinically psychotic individuals with the advent of Zyprexa, Seroquel, and the eagerly awaited Ziprasidone. The Parkinson like tremors, rigidity and stiffness are much less common with these new medications and blood tests are not required. They are much easier to take with few side effects. Although, unfortunately, particularly with Zyprexa, there is a problem with weight gain. Ziprasidone is listed as not causing the Parkinson like side effects nor causing any weight gain. Of course, these antipsychotic drugs are used to treat psychosis. But they are all used to assist in the treatment of depression when the depression is very severe.

When depression becomes severe enough, it is not just a disorder of mood but also a disorder of thought with irrational beliefs and sometimes even hallucinations or delusions developing. A high quality of care requires that an antipsychotic drug be used to help along with the antidepressant when psychotic thinking accompanies a depression. Psychotic thinking may include hearing voices, or severe paranoia. Sometimes these symptoms are not present but the patient may not be able to think in a coherent or logical manner, or perhaps think in such a negative manner, he is not able to function.

Individuals with disorders anywhere along the bipolar spectrum may have significant agitation and irritability. The mood stabilizers begin to kick in after several days or weeks. In the meantime, an antipsychotic drug can be very helpful in decreasing the irritability and agitation and racing thoughts that may occur with any of the bipolar disorders. Now that the safer and easier to use major tranquilizing drugs are available, it is very useful and much less traumatic to add a small dose of a medication such as Zyprexa to the mix to help smooth things over.

Zyprexa (Olanzapine)

Zyprexa first came into use in late 1996 after it was approved by the FDA. This has been one of the more exciting medications over the last several decades. It almost seems like it could be considered a "silver bullet" in treating a lot of psychiatric disorders, and has particular usefulness in the various forms of bipolar disorder. When serious depression exists, there is often a problem with thinking and staying on track, that is when thinking "gets off track" it is often said to be derailed much in the manner of a freight train that jumps the tracks. Zyprexa is one of the newer medications that helps get the train back on track. It also helps slow down the irritability and agitation and does this rather quickly. Most patients notice they are feeling a lot calmer although a little sedated the first few days they are taking Zyprexa. It is also useful in helping with what is known as "negative" symptoms which involve isolation, withdrawal and deterioration that people can get into when they do not take care of themselves very well. Many of the side effects that have been present with some of the more classic antipsychotics such as Haldol, Mellaril, Navane, etc., are much less common with Zyprexa. In the past we had to worry about people getting cramps, tremors, and walking stiffly, but this is actually quite uncommon with Zyprexa.

Although Depakote may very well alleviate the symptoms of mood cycling, particularly irritability and depression, this often takes time, perhaps days to weeks or even months until the maximum benefit is quite evident. However, the Zyprexa may kick in a lot sooner, at least in terms of increasing sedation and helping to bring on sleep and the slowing down of the symptoms of agitation. There does seem to be some anti-mood cycling and antidepressant effect as well as the effect of helping to clear up derailed thinking. Right now it seems quite promising that patients who have not responded well to other antipsychotic medications are now responding well to Zyprexa. The Food and Drug Administration has recently approved Zyprexa for use as an effective treatment for mania in bipolar disorder.

The side effects are remarkably fewer than in the previous anti-psychotic drugs. Physically noticeable is the lack of tremors and muscle stiffness. Unfortunately, a sizeable percentage of individuals will put on weight with Zyprexa. There are other side effects such as sedation and dry mouth, but these are usually fairly well tolerated. The problem with upset stomach does not seem to be as particularly significant as with Depakote. There is an occasional side effect which involves an achey flu-like feeling. The medication should be stopped if this persists.

The maximum dosage recommended by the manufacturer and the FDA is 20 mg per day. However, some physicians are now prescribing more than 20 mg a day in particularly difficult cases. The pills come in various dosage strengths. There are individuals with mild to moderate symptoms who can get by on 5 mg or perhaps as little as 2.5 mg daily. Teenagers can do well on the smaller doses, especially if a firm bipolar diagnosis has not yet been established.

At the present time Zyprexa is a fairly expensive treatment. Each pill costs six to seven dollars and many patients take two pills a day. Over the course of a month that could be four hundred dollars or more, and up to five thousand dollars a year. However, this drug is so effective and relatively safe that, in the long run, it is a lot cheaper than spending a few weeks in the hospital every year.

Seroquel (Quetiapine)

The latest addition to the antipsychotic family, quetiapine, is marketed under the trade name of Seroquel. Supposedly, Seroquel has fewer side effects than any other antipsychotic medication, with little or no stiffness or tremors and less of a weight gain problem. It is fairly sedating which lends it to being very useful as a sleep enhancer without having to rely on addicting medications. Seroquel can be very useful in the early stages of a developing hypomania or mixed state when sleep is beginning to deteriorate. As with Zyprexa, there is a beneficial sedating effect early in treatment, and probably a direct anti-manic effect as well.

There is not much data comparing Seroquel with Zyprexa, although Zyprexa has been around longer, so there is more information confirming its usefulness.

There was some early concern about quetiapine having adverse effects on the eyes since research showed this problem with dogs during the experimental stages. So far, this has not been found to be a problem with humans.

Risperdal (Risperidone)

Risperidone is also one of the novel antipsychotic drugs which is useful and effective for a variety of conditions including acute and maintenance management of bipolar disorders, even if psychotic symptoms are not present. As the other major tranquilizers, it can be quite sedating which makes it useful to aid in sleep, although sometimes it can be activating and energizing. Originally it was touted as not causing the Parkinson like side effects, that is, stiffness, tremors, and shuffling gait. But as it turns out, these symptoms do occur with a moderate degree of frequency.

Chapter Sixteen

Antidepressants and Bipolar Spectrum Disorders

As has been pointed out in the previous chapters and case studies, antidepressants can really cloud the issue when used with patients who have bipolar spectrum disorders. Many people are put on antidepressants after a rather uncritical and cursory evaluation by an overly busy and somewhat distracted physician. The patient is depressed, comes into the clinic complaining of depression, and is put on an antidepressant. Case closed, next patient please. Of course, if this turns out to be a bipolar spectrum disorder, sooner or later it will become obvious that the proper treatment has not been administered. Irritability, agitation and increased mood cycling in response to antidepressants is one of the hallmark clues in defining a bipolar diagnosis. This is especially true when there have been multiple trials of different antidepressants. Antidepressants may be effective for a short while, but soon enough, the house of cards will come tumbling down. Does this mean antidepressants have no place in the treatment of bipolar spectrum disorders? Actually, they do. Basically, the doses need to be low and used in conjunction with other mood stabilizing medications. Unlike routine non-bipolar depressions, the antidepressants should generally be stopped when the mood returns to normal and especially if the mood starts to become a little hyperthymic, that is, the patient starts to feel "better than well." He might like the hyper feeling a little, but still, removing the antidepressant will help take the him out of harm's way.

Following is a brief discussion of some various antidepressants. This is intended only as a basic overview since many thorough and extensive references have been written about these medications elsewhere.

SSRIs

This could also be known as the Prozac family since this was the first and most well known of this new type of antidepressant. When Prozac (fluoxetine) first became available in 1988, it seemed to be a boon for all physicians who prescribed antidepressants. The side effects of these medications seemed to be a lot less than for the previous generation of popular antidepressants known as tricyclic antidepressants. SSRI stands for Selective Serotonin Reuptake Inhibitor. Serotonin is an important chemical in the brain known as a neurotransmitter which helps send signals from one nerve cell to the next. Depletion of serotonin has been implicated in depressions, obsessive compulsive disorders, anxiety disorders, panic attacks, phobias, self injurious behaviors and a number of other symptoms. SSRIs function to make Serotonin available to the nerve cells. Serotonin is one of many neurotransmitters yet one of the most important in treating depression. Although there are several different SSRIs on the market, they have similarities but they are not identical. That means, although the patient may not respond to one of this type of medication, he may respond to a different one. Other than Prozac, the commonly used SSRIs include Paxil, Zoloft, Celexa, and Luvox. Luvox was promoted as the first drug officially approved treating obsessive compulsive disorders (OCD). Most practitioners, however, will use any of the SSRIs to treat OCD. Recently Prozac and Zoloft have been FDA approved to be used for Obsessive Compulsive Disorder.

The SSRIs have been used to treat depression, OCD, social phobias, self injurious behaviors, eating disorders such as bulimia and perhaps anorexia nervosa. Some obsessional habits such as shoplifting, nail biting and hair pulling also can be treated successfully with this class of drugs.

The SSRIs are considered safer to use than some of the other classes of antidepressants for bipolar disorders. They are less likely to cause mood cycling and switching than the tricyclic antidepressants which are discussed below.

Prozac is very long lasting in the body. It can be detected in the blood stream up to two months after the last dose. If a mood switch occurs, stopping Prozac immediately may not help since it is eliminated so slowly. For bipolar patients, I prefer a shorter acting SSRI such as Paxil, just in case a reaction develops.

The side effects include insomnia, especially early in treatment. The patient may report waking up in the middle of the night and not being able to go back to sleep. This seems to fade with time. Another problem which keeps showing up more commonly than originally thought is the sexual side effects. This applies to both men and women and includes difficulty becoming aroused and difficulty having orgasm. These side effects may apply to more than half the patients who take this class of drugs. On occasion, the side effects may be opposite, that is increasing sexual response, which is the exception to the rule. These are not trivial side effects and often lead to the patient discontinuing the medication without consulting the physician. Often the patient does not realize a decrease in sexual activities is related to the drug. There are treatments available which may counteract the sexual side effects, but they are not always reliable. One common treatment is to take the over-the-counter supplement ginko biloba twice daily. If this works, it may take up to a month before it becomes effective.

Some people may gain weight while taking Prozac, but most will maintain their weight and sometimes even lose weight. Weight does not seem to be an overall major problem with the SSRIs although some people have complained of weight gain with Paxil.

Tricyclic Antidepressants (TCAs)

The tricyclic antidepressants are the first generation of antidepressant drugs. They have been around since the mid-1950s and still can be quite effective and useful. They work by a different mechanism than the SSRIs. They enhance the release of various neurotransmitters including serotonin, dopamine, noradrenaline and GABA (Gama Amino Butyric Acid) into the nervous system. They work fairly well and are considered just as effective as the newer SSRIs. However, they tend to have more side effects similar to antihistamines including dryness of mouth, nose and eyes, constipation, dizziness and sedation. Blurring of vision is also common. The common trade names of this class include Elavil (amitriptyline), Tofranil (imipramine), Sinequan (doxepin), and Pamelor (nortriptyline). There are perhaps a dozen others that are used less frequently. They all tend to be quite sedating, requiring a gradual increase in dosage so tolerance to the side effects can develop gradually.

This class of antidepressant is not as widely used in bipolar disorders as are the SSRIs mainly because they are more prone to lead to rapid elevation in mood and may trigger serious cycling and mixed states.

Numerous authorities have recommended combining antidepressants from different classes if one antidepressant alone is not getting the person out of their doldrums. This can be somewhat risky in the bipolar spectrum disorder because the chance of becoming overly activated is increased. As always, however, risks must be assessed and measured against the benefits, and someone who is suicidally depressed may benefit from a lifesaving treatment.

New Generation Antidepressants

There are some new antidepressants which theoretically target more than one neurotransmitter at a time. These newer antidepressants combine the benefit of enhancing serotonin activity and actually function in part as an SSRI, but also affect another important neurotransmitter known as noradrenaline. These new medications theoretically provide a "shotgun effect" in that several targets are being hit at the same time. The three best known of these are Effexor, Serzone, and Remeron.

Effexor has been around the longest and has been shown to be useful in treating anxiety disorders and even attention deficit hyperactivity disorder in adults. It can be particularly activating with bipolar patients. It also has a rather significant amount of sexual side effects as do the pure SSRIs and also tends to cause people to gain weight.

Serzone, although it is promoted as calming the agitated depressed individual, can also cause significant activation in a bipolar depressed patient. One of the strong points, however, is it rarely causes any type of sexual side effects. The same is true for the newer medication Remeron which helps provide a calming effect and rarely has any type of sexual side effects. However, it often causes significant increase in appetite and weight gain.

All of these antidepressants can be used with the bipolar depressed patient, but, again, the dose has to be low and the patient has to be monitored carefully by the prescribing physician.

There are two other special antidepressants which do not fall into any clear category. Wellbutrin has some very specific adrenaline-like activity and shows good antidepressant effect with neither weight gain nor sexual side effects. It has also been credited by some researchers as causing less mood activation with bipolar patients. This tends to be a debatable point and research is somewhat sketchy in this area. There are certainly some bipolar patients who become activated with Wellbutrin and this antidepressant has to be monitored carefully as any other antidepressant medication. It is generally well tolerated without too many side effects, although there has been some concern that high doses may cause seizures and the FDA has required that the manufacturer warn the public of this. Recent studies have shown that the concern about seizures with Wellbutrin may be overstated. The generic chemical name for Wellbutrin is buproprion. Recently it has been approved for marketing under another trade name, Zyban, to help individuals stop smoking. The dosage for helping one to quit smoking is considerably less than the antidepressant dosage.

One other common antidepressant that does not fall into the common categories above is trazadone, also known by the trade name Desyrel. Originally it was tested as a sleeping medication. It is very commonly prescribed by general physicians and sometimes by psychiatrists to help individuals get to sleep and to be taken on an as-needed basis. Small doses in the 25 to 50 milligram range are beneficial in helping people fall asleep. It is often prescribed for sleep because it is not addicting and prescribers tend to be cautious about giving a potentially addicting medication to anyone with a history of substance abuse. Just because an antidepressant is often used for sedating purposes does not mean it is unlikely to cause activation and mood switching in a bipolar patient. Trazadone, which enhances serotonin availability, can cause significant activation. It is a very helpful clue to notice that a patient given trazadone actually ends up getting activated with it.

All of the above antidepressants can be useful in treating depression that occurs in a bipolar spectrum disorder, but care must be taken and mood monitored carefully for signs of switching or developing hyperactivity. Small doses are generally better than large doses and short term use is often better than long term use.

Mono Amine Oxidase Inhibitors (MAO Inhibitors)

MAO inhibitors are antidepressants some practitioners feel are really more potent and useful than other standard antidepressants, whether they are tricyclics or SSRIs. These medications affect a whole host of neurotransmitters and increase their availability and inhibit the enzyme that breaks them down (that's right, the enzyme in mono amine oxidase). There are some bipolar spectrum disorder patients with significant depression who, at times, may respond very well to this type of antidepressant alone. The most common MAO inhibitors are Nardil and Parnate. Even the over-the-counter herbal remedy known as St. John's Wort is a mild MAO inhibitor. Although the MAO inhibitors have been around for many years and are shown to be very effective, they are not used very much because they can be quite troublesome. First of all, they can be very activating, but also there can be a very powerful interaction with other drugs and certain foods that contain the substance tyramine which can also enhance the formation of activating compounds in the body. If the patient taking MAO inhibitors ingests the wrong medication or the wrong food, a reaction can occur which could be anything from a mild headache to a seizure, stroke, or even death. When used in combination with different classes of antidepressants, there is an enhancement of neurotransmitters on one side of the equation and a decrease and breakdown on the other leading to an overload and possibly severe reaction with headache, flushing, and increasing blood pressure. Activating medications such as decongestants, which can be found in cold preparations and cough syrups, could cause a problem as well as asthma medications. Even caffeine usage can cause some degree of reaction. The reactions of eating the wrong kind of food while taking MAO inhibitors are usually mild to moderate, although severe reactions occur. If a reaction is going to occur, it will probably be within minutes of the dietary indiscretion. The worst reaction can occur when there is a concurrent abuse of street drugs such as cocaine or methamphetamine. Sometimes, though, nature works in strange ways. I have seen a patient on the MAO inhibitor Nardil report she had abused amphetamines without even a minor reaction, while a patient who ate an overripe banana had to be rushed to a hospital emergency room.

The most important foods to avoid are preserved, processed foods, particularly pickled herring which would not be much of a sacrifice for most readers. Red wine must also be avoided. The danger from eating the wrong types of foods is often overstated and the list of foods to avoid is really rather modest and does not take any exceptional training. Again, the concept of risks versus benefits has to be carefully considered. A deep seated refractory depression can be a serious, life-threatening condition, and people's lives have been saved by timely intervention with such medication.

There is some controversy as to whether or not MAO inhibitors can be used with other antidepressants. Combinations of antidepressants are sometimes used as noted before. It was once thought that combining an MAO inhibitor with any other type of antidepressant is absolutely prohibited. University centers, and even some brave private practitioners are gradually combining MAO inhibitors with other antidepressants to treat serious resistant depression. There certainly are significant risks involved in such combinations an this should be done only under carefully monitored circumstances.

Chapter Seventeen

Other Medical Treatments

Obviously, there are numerous ways of choosing or combining medications to help an individual with a bipolar spectrum disorder. Sleeping medication is very often an essential part of treatment as noted in the chapter on "Sleep as Treatment." The benzodiazepines or "benzos" or "minor tranquilizers" are discussed elsewhere as well. There are a few other strategies used with varying results. These are briefly mentioned here.

Thyroid Hormone

Thyroid hormone has been used in addition to antidepressants to treat unipolar depression, and there are those now who feel it is very helpful in reducing mood cycling when used in higher dosages. The use of thyroid hormone does not imply the patient has low thyroid functioning. It is just that thyroid hormone is used as a medication to help enhance the mood stabilizers and antidepressant medication. The understanding of the usefulness of thyroid hormone in the treatment of mood cycling disorders is still evolving.

Buspar

Buspirone, known under the trade name Buspar, is an antianxiety agent which has been around since the 1980s. It supposedly is a non-addicting antianxiety agent which takes several weeks to begin working. There are numerous research reports indicating it may be helpful in reducing depression when combined with an antidepressant medication and may also help stabilize mood when used in conjunction with a mood stabilizing agent such as lithium or Depakote. The effectiveness of the use of Buspar in this type of treatment still remains unclear.

Beta Blockers

The beta here refers to a specific nervous system receptor site which is involved in increasing physical activation such as an anxiety or anger response. Beta blockers are good at reducing those physical symptoms such as rapid heartbeat, perspiring, gastrointestinal irritability, shakiness and tremors, etc. Beta blockers have a long and honored history as useful for lowering blood pressure. One particular beta blocker known as Pindolol was thought to be a very good addition to a mood stabilizing regimen. Further research has thrown the usefulness of Pindolol into question as useful for calming down mood cycling. Other well known and useful beta blockers include propranolol (Inderal) and atenolol (Tenormin)

Flax Seed Oil

Flax seed oil can be bought in health food stores, and even at the local supermarket. There does not seem to be any well defined research in this area, although some practitioners swear it does help stabilize moods when taken in dosages of one or two tablespoons a day. Although flax seed oil, which is rich in omega 3 fatty acid, is not even at the true experimental stage yet, this may be the gateway to a nutritional approach to mood disorders. It should be used in conjunction with more conventional treatments.

There has been some considerable interest in general medicine as well as psychiatry about the beneficial use of substances known as omega 3 fatty acids which can be found in certain types of fish such as salmon.

Electroconvulsive Therapy (ECT)

One of the most effective treatments for serious, unremitting depression that does not respond well to medication is ECT. Sometimes this dramatic method of treatment is also used when people suffer from serious agitation or mania. Many people get their impression of how ECT works, and what it does, from movies such as "One Flew Over The Cuckoo's Nest." This movie depicts the state of the art in mental institutions circa the late 1950s. Electroconvulsive therapy is presented as a crude, primitive, and somewhat punitive method of treating patients. But using early Hollywood depictions of ECT as a source of useful information about its use today would be similar to making a decision about surgery by watching the railroad yard scene from "Gone With The Wind."

Still ECT has become a political and social issue as much as a medical issue. It has been around since the 1930s. Over previous decades it has been noted that depressed and schizophrenic individuals often improve after an epileptic seizure. Therefore, some physicians decided to see if causing a seizure in a patient would help reduce mental symptoms. Early seizure therapy involved the use of such substances as camphor and insulin. Ultimately, electricity was found to be the safest and most effective way to treat serious resistant depression.

Surprisingly, ECT is the safest way to treat serious depression and is even safer than using antidepressants which have significant side effects of their own.

Modern methods of administering ECT involve general anesthesia and the patient is put to sleep for just a few minutes during the administration of the electric current. Muscle relaxants are also used so there is really no observable seizure.

When the patient receives an ECT treatment, he may be able to resume reasonably normal activities (except driving, for example) by later in the day.

A pulse of electricity lasting a fraction of a second is sent through the brain causing a seizure which is not apparent to observers. Brain wave activity as noted by an electroencephalogram (EEG) will show what looks like seizure activity for forty-five to ninety seconds. At no time during the procedure or recovery should the patient be uncomfortable.

ECT was used heavily during the 1940s and early 1950s prior to the introduction of modern psychiatric medication. Fortunately, it was very effective and useful. Unfortunately, it was overused and had a lot more problems associated with it since modern methods of anesthesia and muscle relaxation were not used.

It is not exactly clear why ECT works. Recent research supports a theory that the neurotransmitter system in the brain and nervous system are altered through the use of ECT.

Each year, somewhere between 50,000 and 100,000 Americans receive ECT. The most common usage of ECT is for patients with bipolar disorder, particularly Bipolar 1 which is primarily manic depressive illness.

The major side effect of ECT involves memory loss. The memory loss is usually temporary and mild, although more severe and long term cases have been reported. Sometimes it may take several weeks or a month or more for memory to return to normal. The memory loss involves past events and generally does not effect an individual's ability to learn things in the future.

Of course, the prospect of receiving such a treatment can be very anxiety provoking. It requires putting yourself in the hands of a physician or treatment team while you are unconscious. Most clinicians will reserve

ECT as a treatment of last resort. This is a result of the negative press ECT has received. The most common use is for patients who are suicidally depressed, and who may be in danger of losing their lives if they do not receive immediate treatment. Receiving ECT is almost always a voluntary procedure, which means the patient makes the final decision. Proper education will often reduce the fears in patients and their families.

Perhaps one important reason why your depression is not getting better is that a potentially life saving treatment which is humane and safe is often being ignored or discarded based on hysteria and misinformation.

Chapter Eighteen

To Love and to Work

When reflecting upon the essence of mental health, perhaps it was best stated by the distinguished psychoanalyst Theodor Reik, "Work and love-these are the basics. Without them there is neurosis."

This statement is elegant in its simplicity. There is nothing about being "normal" or "happy." A question often asked of psychiatrists is "Who is to say what is normal?" Or for that matter, who is well and who is mentally ill? The task of a psychiatrist is neither to help make people normal or happy, but, in many respects, is similar to the job of any physician, that is, to bring the patient back to a state of health where he or she can function in the world. A person who lives fully in the world is one who has love in his life and is able to be creative, productive, and care for himself the best he can.

Being able to "love" implies the ability to be in meaningful relationships with others. This would include, but not be limited to, a full adult sexualized relationship with an adult partner. It is also the ability to love your children, to love your parents, to be involved with people in your environment and community, to care for and interact with others in a meaningful way. Love, in a broader sense, is a bonding, a connectedness to the people you work with, to the clients you serve and to those who serve you as well. Love is not random sexual encounters nor high levels of dependence on another human being. These are substitutes for true meaning in relationships.

People often have love for their communities, even though the geography and environment may be harsh, it is still home. A sense of place, purpose and belonging are all important elements of the concept of love.

But in order to love, one must feel worthy of being loved and have enough sense of self-esteem to be able to share with others. Some of us are damaged by trauma and illness, and it is the work of the therapist to help that person become whole once again so he or she is able to love and also receive love.

There is love in kindness, love in giving, and love in self sacrifice. And yet, in our society we have developed some very unhealthy notions of what love means. We have become the slaves of popular culture which promotes superficial ideas of who or what is loveable. With the constant bombardment of images of anorectic young models and super stud bad boy athletes, we strive to reach ideals which are destructive and unobtainable.

Generally, the term "work" is used to connote working for a living. But what I believe Freud was talking about was the ability to be creative and productive to the extent one is capable. An artist or a musician may be very creative and productive without really earning very much in the way of money. If an artist has a passion for her work, is able to find a means to support herself while doing her art, then she, indeed, is being very creative and productive. A woman who stays at home and cares for her house and children also works and is productive. The man who volunteers for charity or a political cause is performing work in the very broad sense of the term.

Our working environment has been changing over the last decade. Businesses are downsizing, corporations are becoming "leaner and meaner." Employees are being asked to do more, often with fewer resources. Budgets are trimmed, work forces are reduced. Increased competition among businesses in all sectors of society has led to increased corporate profits and an increase in prosperity. American workers are the most productive in the world. Of course, hard work and dedication are desirable attributes within any culture. We see a trend upward in the number of hours worked and decrease in vacation time. Americans take less vacation than other workers in the industrialized world. The economic machine keeps pumping, but in its wake are the damaged spirits and bodies of those who keep the machine going.

The workplace itself has become manic. It is difficult enough for an individual who has no diagnosable mood disorder to stay even and balanced in a hyperactive culture. The bipolar individual is generally more sensitive to environmental stresses and thus more easily "kindled." The activities of life, loving and working that lead to and also result from a healthy mental state are becoming increasingly difficult and complex. Lithium, Prozac, and the like, although very helpful, are not the prescriptions for the ills of society. Despite the freedoms and bounty of our society, there is also a manic quality and a degree of oppression. We surely can obtain an even higher level of health and stability by obtaining the wisdom to observe and know ourselves. This is really the point of Freud's work.

To remain healthy, the bipolar individual must walk very carefully through the mine fields of our culture. There are many traps and temptations that can lead us to a course of recklessness. One of the most basic and helpful tools for the bipolar patient to maintain healthful living is to continue in some type of psychotherapy. This can be in a group or individual setting. It is particularly important during times of stress, but can also be helpful during periods of relative calm. Most of us do not have superb self observational powers, so that is why we hire a therapist, that is, somebody who observes us and feeds back to us what she sees. The therapist must also be a very healthy individual because someone who is neither wise nor healthy can impart those qualities to someone else. As we have noted elsewhere in this book, stressful circumstances can often ignite or kindle a bipolar episode whether it is hypomania, depression, agitation or a mixture of all of these. The problems are often compounded when an individual makes choices while in a compromised state. A healthy therapist will help provide guidance, make observations about how the patient is doing, whether or not medications need to be adjusted, and help provide guidanceif decisions need to be delayed. Sometimes simple ventilation of feelings can be most calming and therapeutic. The person receiving counseling may ultimately be able to internalize or take in the wisdom and thinking process of the helping therapist. Psychotherapy eventually teaches you to be your own therapist.

It is not unusual for high functioning people with bipolar disorders to want to reject the notion of having an illness and the need to take medications. Unfortunately, during quiet periods when the patient is feeling well, he may very well decide to stop taking the medication, and feel his problem is "cured." One of the tasks of therapy is to learn to deal with and accept the illness that is part of you and to understand you are worthy of love, even when taking your whole humanity into account, including whatever imperfections you may have.

Ultimately, it is important to understand when warning signs occur. When moods begin to swing up or down, it is important to let your physician or therapist know and perhaps avoid a significant period of illness. Many psychiatrists make a good living treating and retreating people who stop their medications when they feel well.

Therapy in a group setting is a good way of connecting with others who may have similar problems and makes it easy to learn by seeing how others cope with the same problems you may have. Group therapy is sometimes rejected as "I don't want to hear other people talk about their problems." But one of the underlying rationales for group therapy is that their problems are also your problems and you can learn a lot about yourself by listening to others in similar circumstances. The mutual support for staying in treatment can be a very powerful tool in helping to maintain a high level of health and functioning.

Know Thyself

Part of the reason for continuing in therapy is the feedback one obtains either from the therapist or other group members. If an individual knows himself and how he feels, he is much better able to check himself and recognize when his moods and activity are starting to get out of control. When irritability and agitation begin to manifest, sometimes the patient himself is the last to know. This is the most essential element of maintaining health. The ancient aphorism "know thyself" can be updated for the bipolar patient as "know thy warning signs." Mild hypomania can feel quite good, especially after a long period of depression. It is often during this time that projects are started that cannot be finished, and promises made that cannot be kept. This is the critical period when people start taking on more and more responsibility, working more hours, sleeping less, and sometimes feeling good about it. Some folks will excuse this as their "Type A behavior" coming forward. The decreasing need for sleep or perhaps just the inability to sleep coupled with increased activity will soon be followed by depression, particularly an agitated depression.

It is more the rule than the exception that the observations of family members are often seen as nagging and end up as being discounted. On the other hand, the feedback of the therapist or other group members can be more valuable, especially when you have seen someone else in the group who originally may have rejected similar feedback.

Stress Managament

There are many things in our lives that we cannot control. The familiar prayer which is the hallmark of humility known as the Serenity Prayer inspires us to know our limitations, that which we can change and that which we cannot. The individual with the bipolar spectrum disorder, through no fault of character, may often have a lower stress tolerance.

That is something that cannot be changed. The concept of kindling implies that increased stress may set off a bipolar episode. Therefore, the bipolar patient, in addition to knowing himself, must also have the ability and good sense to pull back when things become overly stressful. Often, this will require a significant amount of life planning, tradeoffs, and sometimes sacrifices. Some bipolar spectrum patients may function very well during a sustained hyperthymic period; but when the illness evolves into a less functional form, the individual may still try to push herself to perform at previous levels. This is generally a prescription for disaster. The evolution of the illness within the individual, combined with decreased level of functioning as perhaps a bread winner or parent, can lead to further depression and stress. As maturity teaches us, true wisdom and strength can be found in knowing one's limitations and abiding by them. This can be difficult and sometimes even seem impossible when employers, family members, or spouses provide a strong expectation of continued high levels of functioning and productivity. Families must be brought into the circle of treatment because they need education as well.

There are many books and articles on stress management which involve relaxation techniques, breathing techniques, meditation, etc. The bipolar patient has additional demands and limitations and stress management may go beyond the usual techniques and exercises often taught. Actual life changes, including career management and simplification of life style, must often be considered. This is not always easy or practical and sometimes requires retraining. Yet, a failure to do so more often leads to more drastic lifestyle changes by default. A richness of spirit and an increased satisfaction with life can actually be achieved by a carefully planned changing of life. As Fritz Perls once stated, dying one's death and being born again is never easy. This is true, not only for religious experience but also for reinventing oneself in the pragmatic world of day to day living.

Keeping a Rhythm

In the section on seasonal affective disorders, it was noted that it is important, particularly for the bipolar individual, to keep the ebb and flow of the daily cycle at a reasonable and predictable pace. Particularly important is maintaining regularity in sleep pattern. Going to sleep at a certain time and rising at a certain time may help maintain a level of mood and energy stability. Sometimes, if one is beginning to cycle upward, the ability to sleep may move out of your control. This may require medication to assist in maintaining regular sleep on a temporary basis. This does not mean using marijuana and alcohol. Your prescribing physician may very well need to assess your situation and adjust medication so as to provide a good night's sleep when otherwise things would start to race. This would also apply to eating. Grabbing a sandwich or perhaps skipping lunch altogether while on the run is counterproductive. Certainly not everyone has complete control over their schedules. However, skipping breakfast or lunch can become a habit, a very bad habit. It is not just the taking of nutrition that is important, but also the taking of time to sit an take time out from the daily activities and make a meal time a time of respite and enjoyment, even if it is brief.

The rhythm of the work schedule is also important. A regular time of going to work and a regular time of going home helps keep us stable. Working a double shift may be necessary, but it is quite difficult, even for the most stable of individuals. Working rotating shifts is even more difficult and probably should never be done by someone with a bipolar disorder. Remember, anyone with a bipolar disorder is protected by The Americans With Disabilities Act and reasonable accommodations must be made, such as requiring just one routine shift with day shift being the most desirable. People who work night shift will still try to reverse their schedules when they have days off, which is why bipolar patients should be allowed to work primarily a day shift.

It is also good to minimize daytime naps since this may throw off the nighttime sleep regularity. However, sometimes a brief nap, perhaps fifteen minutes, during the day can be very helpful and restful.

Recreation

Notice in the word recreation is the word "creation." When one recreates, one is creating again. The concept of recreation is replenishing that which has been depleted. A competent physician or therapist, or healer of any type knows he cannot give to others unless he has his own resources available.

Think about when you are about to take off in a commercial airplane. The flight attendant will tell you that if the cabin loses pressure, the oxygen masks drop down from the overhead compartment. Who gets the oxygen mask first, you or the child with whom you are traveling? It is surprising that many people believe the child should get the oxygen mask first. But common sense would dictate that you put the oxygen mask on yourself first, allowing you to be clear headed and then fully capable of assisting the child. So it is with your responsibilities as a parent, provider, spouse, teacher, healer, supervisor or any number of roles adults may deal with. Anyone who fancies himself as a workaholic, driving himself, taking on extra tasks, seeing how much business he can negotiate, how many sales he can make, without regard for the elements of his person and physical well being, will sooner or later pay a very dear price. Unfortunately, for bipolar patients, they will very often put themselves in a position of doing just those things. For a time, the energy seems to be there, but still the drive is done at the cost of relationships with others, relaxation and play.

Very often, highly charged people will also play very competitively and lose a sense of perspective. Certainly, it is fun to challenge yourself at times. Training for a marathon, mountain climbing, practicing your golf swing can all be gratifying. But you have to be careful about when it becomes a chore and just another task to be mastered as opposed to pure and honest fun and recreation. Recreation should be just that, recreation and not another stressful event, another task to be mastered.

Children who want to become good at a sport certainly will need to practice. As adults, however, we need to be able to exercise with real enjoyment.

You work hard. You need time to relax and enjoy yourself, not just on Saturday afternoon or evening, but on a day-to-day basis. Sometimes there may be no more than fifteen minutes available, but that fifteen minutes can be very important in helping you to renew and restore yourselves for the next day. It does not have to be anything dramatic, simply reading something you enjoy can be very relaxing and give you something to look forward to at the end of the day.

If working out at the gym starts to become a chore, then perhaps a more relaxing and enjoyable form of exercise should be substituted. If this is done, it is much more likely that you will be able to sustain recreational exercise on an ongoing basis. Running five miles a day may be good for the heart, but so is jogging two miles or even walking for a half hour. The person who criticizes himself as "lazy" because he did not go out and run his five or six miles that night does not really understand what is truly good for him.

Sometimes as hypomania starts to develop, there may be a restlessness that develops. Generally running hard, swimming extra laps, doing a few extra reps on the exercise machine may all feel good and should not be discouraged. But also, if hypomania is developing, this is the time to check with your physician to make sure the developing mood cycling can be managed.

Recreation needs to be part of the flow of day to day living to maintain stability in life. "Easy for you to say. How can I have rest and recreation when I have to work overtime and take care of three screaming kids at home?" you may ask. Well, you may not have time, but if you are a bipolar individual, or even if not, you will soon be running on empty and suffer the consequences. Ultimately, neither the job nor the screaming kids will get the attention they need because you will have crashed and burned. Do not forget to put the oxygen mask on yourself first.

Spirituality

Prayer helps people heal. There is a power higher than ourselves in the universe. There are many different religions in the world from the monotheistic western religions, to the worship of many gods, animals, the land, the sun or the mon. Despite each individual's pathway to God, there is a universal desire to connect somehow to the conscious force behind the universe. Religion, whether highly organized or strictly personal, brings great comfort to many people and, quite often, healing. As humans, we have been able to create the great medications and understand the complexities of the nervous system. Even though we have created these medications, we still do not completely understand how they work. We have been to the moon, but we still do not understand the vast complexities that go on within our skulls and the rest of our bodies. We can make choices, but there are many things we cannot control.

Beyond the therapy, the medications, the charts and graphs, and the medical diagnoses, is another presence. This is not a discussion about focusing life on religious belief, but a suggestion that making room in your heart for a presence greater than yourself, will ultimately provide comfort and healing for you and the ones you love.

About the Author

Michael R.Bartos is a psychiatrist currently working with Kaiser Permanente in Vallejo, California. He is also the chief of staff at California Specialty Hospital in Vallejo. Previously he has held clinical faculty positions with Penn State University, the Medical University of South Carolina, and Napa State Hospital in California.

Glossary

ACTIVATION: A marked and usually sudden increase in
               the level of energy, either physical or men-
               tal usually caused by the taking of a med-
               ication or other substance.

ADHD: Also known as attention deficit hyperac-
               tivity disorder. This is most commonly
               diagnosed in childhood but can last into
               adulthood. It is characterized by hyperac-
               tivity, unstable moods, inability to focus
               and concentrate and often accompanied
               by mild to moderate learning disabilities
               and sometimes mild physical problems
               including lack of coordination.

AGITATED
DEPRESSION: A mood state characterized by a
               depression, also mild to moderate
               hyperactivity and irritability. Originally,
               this was thought to be a separate type of
               depression, but appears to actually be a
               characteristic of bipolar spectrum disorder
               in which depression and activation are
               present at the same time.

ANTIDEPRESSANT: Any one of a number of several different
                 classes of medication which are designed
                 specifically to reduce the symptoms of

depression. The more common classes of antidepressants include tricyclic antidepressants (TCAs), Serotonin Selective Reuptake Inhibitors (SSRIs) and Monamine Oxidase Inhibitors (MAOIs).

ANTIPSYCHOTIC: Medications which are prescribed specifically to reduce the symptoms of psychosis. They are generally prescribed to reduce disorders of thinking and perception, especially hallucinations, paranoia, and sometimes ruminative or repetitive thinking and intrusive thoughts. They are also useful in reducing agitation that accompanies manic states and also the agitation that appears with severe depression.

BENZODIAZEPINES: This class of drugs is also known as minor tranquilizers and antianxiety agents. This includes medications that are related such as Valium, Ativan, Klonopin, Xanax, and several other commonly known agents. There are some sleeping pills which also belong in this class including Restoril and Dalmane. These medications are very useful in reducing anxiety very quickly and can be very helpful when someone has irritability which may accompany a bipolar disorder. Sometimes these medications are used for mild to moderate anxiety caused by the stresses of daily living. They are generally quite useful medications, but also can be very habit forming, especially when used on a day-to-day basis. Since benzodiazepines act at similar receptor sites in the nervous system as does alcohol, these medications can be used to help alcoholics through withdrawal.

BIPOLAR SPECTRUM
DISORDER:

Any one of a number of mood disorders which involves Instability of moods with cycles between agitated states and subdued or depressed states. The characteristic feature is mood cycling, although there are many variations in the way moods will rise and fall. Manic depression is only one of the bipolar spectrum disorders, known as Bipolar Type I. Other disorders can present primarily as highly activated energetic states and some present as deep withdrawn depression. Certain bipolar spectrum disorders have a varying level of mixture of the moods.

BORDERLINE PERSONALITY
DISORDER:

This term is used to describe individuals with characterologic disorders which can encompass a variety of symptoms and behaviors including chronic agitated depression, chaotic interpersonal relationships, self injurious behaviors, and often associated with substance abuse. Such individuals frequently express dramatic and demanding behaviors.

CIRCADIAN RHYTHMS: This refers to the daily rhythm of life functions of humans and other living animals and plants. It involves the sleep cycle, energy levels, and the rhythmic rise and fall of various hormones in the body.

COMPULSIVE SPENDING: A chronic habit of spending that usually derives from boredom or sometimes an obsessive need to own things or shop. The compulsive spender usually has a long time habit of spending to receive personal gratification which may be missing elsewhere in life.

CYCLING: The up and down variation of moods that can occur particularly in an individual with a bipolar spectrum disorder. Cycles are rarely even or smooth.

CYCLOTHYMIA: A bipolar disorder characterized by intermittent periods of depression and other periods of increased energy or activation but of a lower level of intensity than true manic depression.

DEPRESSION: A mood state involving a variety of symptoms including sleep disturbance, appetite disturbance, low energy, poor self esteem, and a decreased level of functioning. This is differentiated from sadness which is a normal human emotion. Sadness does not generally imply a decreased level of functioning on an ongoing basis, whereas depression can be a condition which leads to diminished function in many areas including career, relationships, and general enjoyment of life. As the term implies, depression means a lowering of mood state. Sometimes irritability and agitation can accompany a depression and this may be an important clue in diagnosing a bipolar spectrum disorder. Suicidal thinking or behavior is characteristic of severe depression.

DOPAMINE:

One of numerous chemicals in the brain which transmits impulses form one nerve ending to the next. Disorders of dopamine transmission are implicated in depression and certain thought disorders. Dopamine can also transmit pleasurable impulses. Most of the original antipsychotic medications help to correct certain defects in dopamine transmission in the brain. Low levels of dopamine are thought to cause Parkinson's Disease.

DSM IV:

The Diagnostic and Statistical Manual Fourth Edition of the American Psychiatric Association. This book lists the criteria for psychiatric diagnoses and also describes the various symptoms and syndromes that make up the basic classifications of various psychiatric disorders. This is sometimes referred to as the "Bible" of psychiatric diagnosis.

DYSTHYMIA: Chronic low grade depression. This sometimes does not meet the actual DSM IV criteria for major depression, but dysthymia can cause ongoing problems with ability to function on a day-to-day basis.

FDA: Food and Drug Administration. This is an agency of the Federal Government which approves medications for sale and use in the United States.

FLIGHT INTO HEALTH: The rather rapid and sometimes surprising change from depression to a rather cheerful state sometimes within a day of the initiation of treatment. Originally, this was thought to be the patient's attempt to deny symptoms by pretending to be healthy. However, it also seems that antidepressants may cause a rapid change of mood from serious depression into cheerful elation. It appears that this phenomenon may be related to individuals with bipolar depression who are switching moods rapidly because of the activating property of an antidepressant.

GABA: Gama Amino Butyric Acid. One of numerous chemicals in the brain known as neurotransmitters. GABA has a calming and inhibitory effect. Defects or decreases in GABA can lead to depressions or mania.

HYPOMANIA: A state of increased energy often accompanied by elevated mood. There may also be some irritability and pressured speech as well. Although this is an increased level of energy, it is not full blown mania and is not accompanied by psychotic symptoms.

HYPOSOMNIA:

A state of requiring less than the usual amount of sleep. Sometimes an individual may feel very well on two or three hours of sleep per night, at other times the individual would like to sleep more but is just not able to. Periods of hyposomnia can go on for several days or weeks. This is characteristic of individuals with a bipolar spectrum disorder.

HYPERTHYMIA:

Often this is a personalty state which is characterized by increased energy, decreased need for sleep, and ongoing high levels of productiveness. An individual may be hyperthymic for many years without really cycling into depression. However, hyperthymia is often a precursor to a mood cycling state which may eventually develop.

INTRUSIVE
THOUGHTS:

Thoughts of a worrisome nature, and are usually quite negative which enter into a person's consciousness, even though the individual desires not to have them there. When an individual is significantly depressed, there may be intrusive thoughts about suicide, hurting oneself, or hurting others. Usually these thoughts are very unpleasant and the individual wishes he did not have them. Even though the thoughts are there, generally the patient tries very hard not to act out on these thoughts. This is also seen in obsessive compulsive disorders.

IMPULSIVE SPENDING: This involves spending sprees which are otherwise uncharacteristic for the individual involved in this behavior. This differs from compulsive spending in that the compulsive spender is generally involved in ongoing habitual spending. Impulsive spending often leads to significant financial problems and degradation of one's credit rating. Episodic spending sprees are characteristic of individuals going through an activation phase of a bipolar spectrum disorder.

INSOMNIA: A period of inability to sleep. This differs from hyposomnia in that insomnia is always distressing to the patient and generally harmful. Hyposomnia is not always distressing and very often the individual can feel relatively well during ongoing periods of a decreased need for sleep.

KINDLING: The process of activating an episode of agitation and/or depression. Also, kindling implies the predisposing of the nervous system to developing episodes of depression or agitation. For example, trauma in early life can predispose the brain to be more susceptible to episodes of depression or agitation in later life. Psychotic or bipolar episodes also can cause an individual to become more susceptible to further episodes later in life. Psychological trauma or stress can, therefore, "kindle" a susceptible nervous system into developing a serious psychiatric episode.

MAJOR DEPRESSIVE
DISORDER:

Serious symptomatic depression. It can occur once in a lifetime or occur many times. It is characterized by physical and psychological symptoms which lead to a significant deterioration in functioning. There are specific DSM IV criteria for major depressive disorder. To be diagnosed as a manic depressive, an individual must have had at least one episode of major depressive disorder somewhere in his past. Symptoms include appetite and sleep disturbance, decreased levels of functioning and activity and is often accompanied by suicidal thoughts or behaviors. In more serious forms of major depressive disorder there is also psychotic or distorted thinking.

MAJOR
TRANQUILIZER:

Another name for the antipsychotic drugs.

MANIA:

A state of markedly increased energy both physical and mental. There is characteristic irritability, agitation, sometimes combativeness, sometimes grandiose delusions. The individual is in a very hyper and agitated state. He may be very euphoric, generally very talkative and very often psychotic and not making sense. A manic individual is often out of touch with reality and unfortunately does not realize he has a very serious condition which requires immediate treatment.

MAO INHIBITOR

Also known as Mono Amine Oxidase Inhibitor, a potent class of antidepressant which can be very effective when other antidepressants fail. They act by inhibiting an enzyme which helps break down neurotransmitters. Although very effective, they have a drawback of requiring certain dietary restrictions because of chemical reactions which can cause severe side effects. There are also a lot of drug interactions which can cause serious reactions as well. The dietary restrictions are usually not very difficult to follow and most patients do not run into difficulty because of dietary indiscretions. These can be very useful for patients who have not responded well to other medications, but should be reserved for very motivated and alert patients.

MIXED STATE: In bipolar disorders, a condition where depression in the manic or hypomanic state essentially occur at the same time. This is classically perceived as what is known as "agitated depression," that is, a condition where depression is combined with a state of activation and irritability. It is not a paradox or contradiction to be depressed and mildly manic at the same time. This is quite common in bipolar spectrum disorders, and can be a very dangerous state whereby a depressed patient develops the level of irritability and energy sufficient to carry out a suicide attempt.

MOOD STABILIZER: One of a variety of medications used to treat bipolar spectrum disorders. Although not specifically antidepressants, they have good effect in reducing depression and preventing it from recurring. They also help keep the manic or hypomanic states from recurring as well. The best known of these medications is lithium, but some are as useful if not more useful and include Depakote, Tegretol, Lamictal, and Neurontin. A new anticonvulsant which is used as a mood stabilizer known as Topamax holds some promise as well.

MOOD SWITCH: A rapid change in mood usually from depression to cheerfulness, hypomania, or even mania. This usually occurs when a bipolar individual takes an antidepressant and is quickly activated from the depressed state to the hyperactive state.

MEDICAL MODEL: A model of defining illness which involves diagnosis, treatment, doctors and patients.

MINOR
TRANQUILIZERS: A commonly used term for benzodiazepines.

MORBIDITY: Injury, or decreased functioning that arises out of an illness. This can also refer to accident or injury that occurs from medical treatment itself.

MORTALITY: A death that results from illness or accident.

NEUROLEPTIC: Another term for antipsychotic drug or major tranquilizer. The term derives from its presumed effect on the nervous system.

NEUROTRANSMITTER: Anyone of the dozens of chemicals that transmit messages from one nerve cell to another. The most common neurotransmitters dealt with in psychiatry are Serotonin, Dopamine, GABA (Gama Amino Butyric Acid) and Noradrenaline.

NORADRENALINE: An activating neurotransmitter. Medications that affect the Noradrenaline system are referred to as Noradrenergic.

OCD: Obsessive compulsive disorder. A condition characterized by frequent, intrusive or repetitive thoughts (obsessions). Often these thoughts are very disturbing and unwanted. Beyond the obsessions are the compulsions which involve the actual physical activity of involving oneself in rituals, excessive cleanliness, hand washing, straightening up, or checking. There are also variations which involve other compulsive behaviors such as nail biting, hair pulling, or frequent repetitive sexual activity, or eating disorders such as bulimia.

OFF LABEL:
The use of a medication for something other than the usage approved for by the FDA. Even though the FDA does not approve a specific usage of drug, if that drug is legal and on the market, it may be used for many other purposes which will be legal as well. The best example is the use of antiepileptic or anticonvulsant drugs for the purpose of mood stabilization. Although this is not an FDA approved usage, it is accepted by the medical and psychiatric community and is considered good medical practice.

PARKINSONISM:
A nervous system disorder characterized by tremors, stiffness, and difficulty walking. Sometimes there is also a blank or staring facial expression and sometimes difficulty thinking. There are various neuroleptics which bring on Parkinsonism as well because of their effect on the Dopamine neurotransmitter system. Fortunately,

these Parkinson like symptoms are reversible once the medication is stopped or additional medications to control the side effects are added.

POLYPHARMACY: The use of numerous medications in combination in order to treat a condition for which one medication alone would be inadequate. Bipolar disorder often requires more than one medication to provide stabilization. Polypharmacy is accepted and perhaps even expected in the treatment of bipolar disorders.

PSYCHIATRIST: A physician who treats mental disorders.

PSYCHOLOGIST: An individual with academic training in the understanding and treatment of mental disorders, but who is not a physician.

PSYCHOSOCIAL MODEL: The understanding and treatment of a mental disorder in terms of life experiences and environment on current behavior. Individuals treated in this model are referred to as "clients" who seek treatment from a therapist or counselor.

PSYCHOSIS: A state of altered thinking, reality, and perception. Psychotic individuals are often thought of as being "out of touch with reality." During a period of psychosis, an individual may be very paranoid, may hallucinate, may see or hear things other people don't see, may believe he has special powers or believe falsely that he is being persecuted or spied upon. There may be a set of beliefs that are very bizarre. Sometimes psychosis is characterized by the inability to compete or express thoughts. A psychotic individual may have a belief system or perceptions that a reasonably clear thinking person would be able to see as false or bizarre. Psychosis can be chronic or, as in the case of an individual experiencing a manic episode, very acute and treatable and resolve over time with proper treatment.

RAPID CYCLING: A state of quick movement between moods. In classic manic depression, moods go from depressed to manic and depressed again over the course of several months. An individual with rapid cycling may move through mood states quickly, perhaps in the course of weeks, or even within days or perhaps even hours. Patients with rapid cycling are prone to develop agitated depressions.

REFRACTORY: Resistant to treatment.

SEROTONIN: One of the neurotransmitters which, when depleted, leads to serious depression. Serotonin imbalances are also indicated in obsessive compulsive disorder, bulimia and many anxiety disorders.

SSRI:

Serotonin Selective Reuptake Inhibitor. A medication which enhances the availability of Serotonin in the nervous system. Such medications include Prozac, Paxil, Zoloft, Luvox and Celexa.

SUBSTANCE ABUSE:

The recreational use of various street drugs, alcohol, or perhaps even prescription medications in order to achieve an enjoyable effect. This ften leads to addiction and deterioration of the personality and functioning of the abuser.

SUBSTANCE MISUSE:

The behavior here is similar to that of substance abuse except the individual is using alcohol, or other drugs in order to self treat abnormal mood states such as depression or agitation. Very often the substance misuser will not enjoy the use of these various substances.

TRICYCLIC ANTIDEPRESSANTS
(TCA):

The original medications used to treat depression and are still in use today. They are so named because of the appearance of the chemical structure of these drugs. Included in this category of medications are Elavil, Tofranil, Sinequan, Pamelor, and Norpramine. This class of medications tends to be quite effective, although there tend to be more side effects than the SSRIs.

UNIPOLAR:

Depression which can occur as a single episode or repetitive episode. The symptoms may be significant enough to qualify for major depressive disorder. However, there is no definitive mood cycling associated with unipolar depression.

Bibliography

Akiskal, Hagop; The Bipolar spectrum: new concepts in classification and diagnosis. In: Grinspoon, L, ed. Psychiatry Update: The American Psychiatric Association Annual Review. Washington: American Psychiatric Press: 1983.

Akiskal, HS, Djenderdjian,AH, Rosenthal, RH, Khani, MK; Cyclothymic disorder: validating criteria for inclusion in the bipolar affective group. American Journal of Psychiatry. 1977; 134(11): 1227-1233. Z

Akiskal, Hagop; The prevalent clinical spectrum of bipolar disorder: Beyond DSM IV. Journal of Clinical Psychopharmacology, 1996;16(suppl 1)45ff.

Akiskal, Hagop; Temperment. personality, and depression in Research in Mood Disorders: an Update, Hogrefe and Huber publishers,1994.

Akiskal, Hagop; The Milder spectrum of bipolar disorders: diagnostic, characterologic, and pharmacologic aspects. Psychiatric Annals, 17:33-37, 1987

Akiskal, Hagop; Mood disorders in the Merck Manual for Diagnosis and Therapy, 16th ed. 1992;1593-1619.

Alterman,AJ, Petrarule,E, Tarter,RE, Mcgowan, JR; Hyperactivity and alcoholism: familial and behavioral correlates. Addictive Behaviors, 1982;7(4) 413-421.

American Psychiatric Association. Practice guidelines for the treatment of patients with bipolar disorder. American Journal of Psychiatry. 1994; 15(12) supplement.

Baker, Barbara; Consider shifting drugs quickly in bipolar mania. Reported in Clinical Psychiatry News, December 1998; 12.

Bhandary, A, et al; Pharmacotherapy in adults with ADHD. Psychiatric Annals 1997;27(8); 545-555.

Biederman, J; Developmental subtypes of bipolar disorder. Sexual and Marital therapy. 1995; 3(4) 227-228.

Biederman, J, Faraone, S, Mick, E, Wozniak, J, et al; Attention Deficit disorder and juvenile mania: an overlooked comorbidity? Journal of Child and Adolescent Psychiatry. 1996;35(8) 997-1008.

Borchardt, CM, Bernstein, GA; Comorbid disorders in hospitalized bipolar adolescents compared with unipolar depressed adolescents. Child Psychiatry and Human Development, 1995; 26(1) 11-18.

Bowden, CL; The clinical appoach to the differential diagnosis of bipolar disorder. Psychiatric Annals, 1993;23(2): 57-63.

Brady, KT, Sonne, SC; The Relationship between substance abuse and bipolar disorder. Journal of Clinical Psychiatry. 1995;56(3):118-123.

Brady, KT, Casto,S, Lydiard, RB, et al; Substance abuse in an inpatient psychiatric sample. American Journal of Drug and Alcohol abuse.1991; 17;389-397

Calabrex, JR, et al: A double blind placebo controlled study of lamotrigene monotherapy in outpatients with bipolar I depression. The Journal of Clinical Psychiatry, 1999;60(2):79-88.

Casat, C; The Under and overdiagnosis of mania in children and adolescents. Comprehensive Psychiatry, 1982; 23(6) 552-569.

Chekov, Anton; Anton Chekov's Short Stories, Ralph Motlan,-editor. W.W Norton & Co. 1977.

Chen, Y, Dilsover, S; Comorbidity for obsessive compulsive disorder in bipolar and unipolar disorders. Psychiatry Research, 1995; 59(1-2): 57-64.

Diagnostic and Statistical Manual of Mental Disorders, Fourth Edition. American Psychiatric Association, 1994.

Duke, Patty, Hochman, Gloria; A Brilliant Madness; Living with Manic Depressive Illness. Bantam Books, 1993.

Dumas, Lynne S; Altered states: one extreme breeds another. Health, April, 1988; 20(4) p 20.

Dunner, DL; Lithium carbonate: maintenance studies and consequences of withdrawal. Journal of Clinical Psychiatry, 1998; 59(supplement 6):48-55.

Fawcett, Jan; on the Prevalence of bipolar disorders in the Bipolar Disorders Letter, August 1997; page 8.

Frank, Ellen; Disruption in sleep may lead to mania in bipolar disorder, presented at The Second International Conference of Bipolar Disorders. 1997.

Gibran, Kahlil; The Prophet, Alfred A. Knopf, New York, 1923.

Gold, Mark S; The Good News About Depression. Bantam, Doubleday, Dell Publishing Group, 1987.

Goldberg, JF, Harrow, M, Grossman, LS; Recurrent affective syndromes in bipolar and unipolar mood disorder at followup. British Journal of Psychiatry, 1995; 166(3) 382-385.

Goldberg, JF, Harrow, M, Grossman, LS; Course and outcome in bipolar affective disorder, a longitudinal followup study. American Journal of Psychiatry, 1995; 152(3) 379-389.

Goodwin, FK, Jamison, KR; Manic Depressive Illness. New York, Oxford University Press; 1990.

Heit,MD, Nemeroff, CB; Lithium augmentation in treatment refractory depression. Journal of Clinical Psychiatry,1998; 59(supplement 6): 23-28.

Isaac, G; Is bipolar disorder the most common diagnostic entity in the hospital? Adolescence, 1995; 30(118) 273-276.

Johnson, S, Roberts, JE; Life events and bipolar disorder; Implications from biological theories. Psychological Bulletin, 1995; 117(3): 434-449.

Kaplan, H, Sadock, B; Synopsis of Psychiatry, Williams and Wilkins, Baltimore, 1998.

Keck, PE, McElroy, S; Current Perspective on treatment of bipolar disorder with Lithium. Psychiatric Annals, 1993; 23(2)

Keck, PE, McElroy, SE, Strakowski, SM; Anticonvulsants and antidepressants in the treatment of bipolar disorder. Journal of Clinical Psychiatry, 1998; 59(supplement 6): 74-81.

Klerman, GL; The Classification of bipolar disorders, Psychiatric Annals,1987;17(1)13-17

Kopacz, DR, Janicak, PG: The relationship between bipolar disorder and personality. Psychiatric Annals, 1996; 26(10)

Kutcher, SP, Morton, P, Rosenblum, M; Relationship between psychiatric illness and conduct disorder in adolescents. Canadian Journal of Psychiatry, 1989; 34(6): 526-529.

Leibenluft, E; Gender issues in treating bipolar disorder. Interview in Psychiatric Times. May 1998(Supplement 1) 4-7.

Lish, JD; The National Depressive and Manic Depressive Association survey of bipolar members. Journal of Affective Disorders. 1994: 31(4):281-294.

McCance-Katz, EF, Leal, J, Schottenfeld, RS; Attention deficit hypeactivity disorder and cocaine abuse. American Journal of Addiction, 1995; 4(1):88-91.

Orsillo, SM, Weathers, FW, Litz, BT, Steinberg, HR, et al; Current and lifetime disorders among veterans with war zone related posttraumatic disorders. Journal of Nervous and Mental Disease, 1996; 184(5):307-313.

Physicians Desk Reference, Medical Economics Data Production Company.

Pies, Ronald, editor; Assessing the value of atypical antipsychotics and enhancing the risk benefit ratio. Supplement to the Psychiatric Times, February, 1999.

Pies, Ronald, editor; Improving therapeutic outcomes in bipolar disorder. Psychiatric Times, 7 (supplement 2)

Pliszka, SR; Comorbidity of attention deficit hyperactivity disorder with psychiatric disorder: an overview. Journal of Clinical Psychiatry 1998:59 (supplement 7):50-58.

Post, RM; Treatment Resistant Bipolar Disorder: Research, Pharmacologic Approaches, as quoted in the Bipolar Disorders Letter, February, 1998.

Post, RM, Rubinow, DR, Ballenger, JC; Conditioning and sensitization in the longitudinal course of affective illness. British Journal of Psychiatry, 1986;149: 191-201.

Potter, W; Bipolar depression: specific treatments. Journal of Clinical Psychiatry, 1998;59 (supplement 18):30-36.

Regier, DA, Farmer, ME; Comorbidity of mental disorders with alcohol and other drug abuse. Results from the Epidemiological Catchment Area Study. Journal of the American Medical Association, 1990; 264: 2511-2518.

Sachs, G; Treatment Algorithms and polypharmacy for bipolar disorder. Quoted in the Bipolar Disorder Letter, 1995; 1(4): 3-4.

Savin, M, Perugi, G, Simonimi, E, Soriani, A; Affective comorbidity in panic disorder: is there a bipolar connection? Journal of Affective Disorders, 1993;28(3):155-163.

Schatzberg, AF; Bipolar Disorder: recent issues in diagnosis and classification. Journal of Clinical Psychiatry, 1998; 59(Supplement G): 5-10.

Schubiner, H, et al; Prevalence of attention deficit hyperactivity disorder and conduct disorder among substance abusers, Journal of Clinical Psychiatry, 2000;61:244-251.

Shaffer, D; Diagnosing attention deficit hyperactivity disorder in adults. American Journal of Psychiatry, 1994; 151(5):633-638.

Sherman, Carl; CBT Gains Favor for treating bipolar Disorder. March, 1999; p18.

Simpson, James B, Editor; Simpson's Contemporary Quotations, Harper Collins, 1996.

Skodol, AE, Gallaher, PE, Oldham, JM; Excessive dependency and depression: Is the relationship specific? Journal of Nervous and Mental Disease, 1996; 184(3):16-17.

Stowe, ZN; Selected topics pertaining to postpartum psychiatric disorders. Interview in Currents in Affective Illness, 1996;15(5):5-8.

Strakowski, SM, McElroy, SL, Keck, PW, West, SA; The co-occurrence of mania with medical and other psychiatric disorders. International Journal of Psychiatry in Medicine, 1994; 24(4):305-328.

Sussman, N; Background and rationale for use of anticonvulsants in psychiatry. Cleveland Clinic Journal of Medicine, 1998;65 (supplement 1):7-14.

Swann, AC, et al; Depression during mania: treatment and response to lithium or divalproex. Archives of General Psychiatry, 1997;54:37-42.

Webster's New Collegiate Dictionary, G&C Merriam Company, Springfield, MA.

Weller, EB, Weller, DA, Fristad, MA; Bipolar disorders in children. Journal of the Academy of Child and adolescent Psychiatry, 1995; 34(6):709-714.

Wender, Paul; Attention deficit hyperactivity disorder in adults: a wide view of a widespread condition. Psychiatric Annals 1997; 27(8): 556-562.

West, SA, McElroy, SL, Strakowski, SM, Keck, PE; Attention deficit hyperactivity in adolescent mania. American Journal of Psychiatry, 1995; 152(2):271-273.

West, SA, Strakowski, SM, Sax, KW, Minney, KL, et al; The comorbidity of attention deficit hyperactivity disorder in adolescent mania: potential diagnostic and treatment implications. Psychopharmacology Bulltin, 1995; 31(2):347-351.

West, SA, Strakowski, SM, Sax, KW, McElroy, S, et al; Phenomonology and comorbidity of adolescents hospitalized for the treatment of acute mania. Biological psychiatry, 1996; 39(6): 458-460.

Whybrow, Peter; Bipolar disorder survey, presented at the convention of the American Psychiatric Association. May 1993.

Wilens, TE, Biederman, J, Spencer, TJ, Prince, J; Pharmacotherapy of adult attention deficit disorder: a review. Journal of Clinical Psychopharmacology, 1995: 15(4):270-279.

Winokur, G, Coryell, W, Akiskal, HS, et al; Alcoholism in manic depressive illness: familial illness, course of illness, and the primary-secondary distinction. American Journal of Psychiatry, 1995;152:365-372.

Winokur, G, Coryell, W, Endicott, J, Akiskal, H; Further distinctions between manic depressive illness and primary depressive disorder. American Journal of Psychiatry, 1993;150(8) 1176-1181.

Wozniak, J, Biederman, J, Kiely, K; Mania-like symptoms suggestive of childhood onset bipolar disorder in clinically referred children. Journal of the American Academy of Child and Adolescent Psychiatry, 1995;34(7):867-876.

Index